Causey
(1853–1946)

George Alexander and his family
at Causeyport Farm, Portlethen

by Alan Jamieson

Edited by
Ivor Normand

ISBN: 1-900173-89-1

First published 2004

Published by
Aberdeen & North-East Scotland Family History Society

Printed by
Rainbow Enterprises, Howe Moss Crescent, Kirkhill Industrial Estate, Dyce, Aberdeen

*Dedicated
to my wife,
Maxine*

Contents

Illustrations

George Alexander ("Causey", 1853–1946), in 1931, leaving the Joint Station in Aberdeen to attend a reunion of Queen Victoria's "Volunteers" on the 50th anniversary of the "Wet Review" in Edinburgh. This portrait of Causey appeared in *The Bulletin* newspaper.

Introduction

As a nonagenarian, my grandfather, George Alexander ("Auld Causey", 1853–1946), recalled much about his early days. He havered on at length. Sadly, it seems that his comments went unrecorded at the time. Although I cannot hope to reproduce his memories, I can at least record my own impressions of the man, his wife, their family and their farm as I knew them. I have also drawn on the memories of my sisters and of some of my cousins, to all of whom I am grateful. In the pre-tractor days, the lives of the workers on the farms had more in common with their great-great-grandfathers than with those of the subsequent generation.

Another reason for writing is that part of the Causeyport farm steading was destroyed by fire but has been rebuilt and modernised by the present farmer, Mr Alexander Shand. I describe the house and steading as I remember them, and relate some biographical facts and anecdotes about the character and lifestyle of the now deceased generation of the Alexander family who were reared at Causeyport Farm, Portlethen, where I was a temporary loon, an ignorant toonser fae Aiberdeen. The Alexanders lived at Causeyport from 1904 to 1943, before the Grants and now the Shands.

But first, I should explain my limited qualification for this statement. I lived with my parents Sam Jamieson and Ann (born Alexander) in Aberdeen from birth in 1927 up to conscription from 1945–8, and returned as a student from 1948–52. I then moved south, so I am less familiar with changes since 1952. During those early years, I visited relatives on my mother's side at Causeyport Farm, at "Lochnagar", Muchalls, at Glithno Farm just off the Netherley road out of Stonehaven, and at Dryden Cottage, Stonehaven. These notes are forever incomplete; I can only relate my impressions, and have recorded odd bits of information from memory. I am glad that several relatives have taken the trouble to challenge my havering, and I gratefully acknowledge their contributions. I thank especially my sisters Anne, Isobel and Edith, and my cousins Eunice, John, Audrey, Helen ("Babs"), Pat, George, Sandy, Laura and Ivor the editor for lots of help.

Genealogy

My late parents, uncles, aunts, grandparents, great-grandparents and numerous other relatives are commemorated on stones in the kirkyards at Portlethen and Banchory-Devenick. On genealogy, I defer to my first cousin once removed, Ivor Normand, who has made a meticulous ongoing study of the distribution of the Alexander and Ritchie families and their antecedents and descendants, as far back as records permit. My notes supplement some members of generations "5" and "6" (see explanation in Tables 1–3 below). Ivor can be contacted at 14 Montague Street (3F1), Edinburgh EH8 9QX (0131-667 6860; ivor1hbt@tesco.net).

Alan Jamieson
June 2004

"The Pleasance", 35 Cotmer Road, Oulton Broad, Suffolk NR33 9PL   01502 572653   ajamie@dircon.co.uk

1

Portlethen

Way of life

Portlethen is a village on the Kincardineshire coast of North-East Scotland, about six miles south of Aberdeen. The land in the area continues to support mixed farming. Longshore fishing was once the main activity of the inhabitants of the three coastal villages, namely Findon, Portlethen and Downies. It is said that the internationally acclaimed "finnan haddie" curing process originated in Findon. There appeared to be two distinctive indigenous populations, the fishers and the farmers. The fishers and farmers met at school and in the kirk, but the distinctive skills of seamanship and agriculture kept the two communities apart. The families of fishermen were required to weave and mend nets, bait long lines, gut, fillet, cure and smoke fish. The fishwives trudged the roads selling fish from wicker creels, which they carried on their backs. Farmers' wives milked cows, made butter and cheese, tended calves, reared and fed poultry, and collected and packed eggs. Some farming wives transported and sold their produce on the Green in Aberdeen on Friday market day. The women had a rough deal, but those I remember were well able to fend for themselves. Certain surnames were exclusive to one or other lifestyle. For example, the names Craig and Main occurred so frequently in the fishing villages that house numbers were added to commonly occurring names in the schoolroom. Until recently, the scatter of familiar regional surnames in the local farming community did not suggest immigration.

Portlethen annual picnic and show

As I remember, the Portlethen Picnic in the 1930s was a well-supported annual event centred on the Jubilee Hall, Portlethen, and occupying an adjoining field, which now supports dwelling houses. The construction of the hall in 1887 was financed from the proceeds of penny concerts, at which the young George Alexander (later "Causey") was a popular singer and entertainer. Obviously, he was not then the irascible old man supporting himself on two walking-sticks, except of course when acting that part. Participation and competition, fun and games, were the

Portlethen Picnic, c. 1925 (box camera). Left to right: Margaret Hay Alexander, Samuel Jamieson (author's father), Ann Paterson Alexander (author's mother), George Gray, Jessie Brechin Alexander.

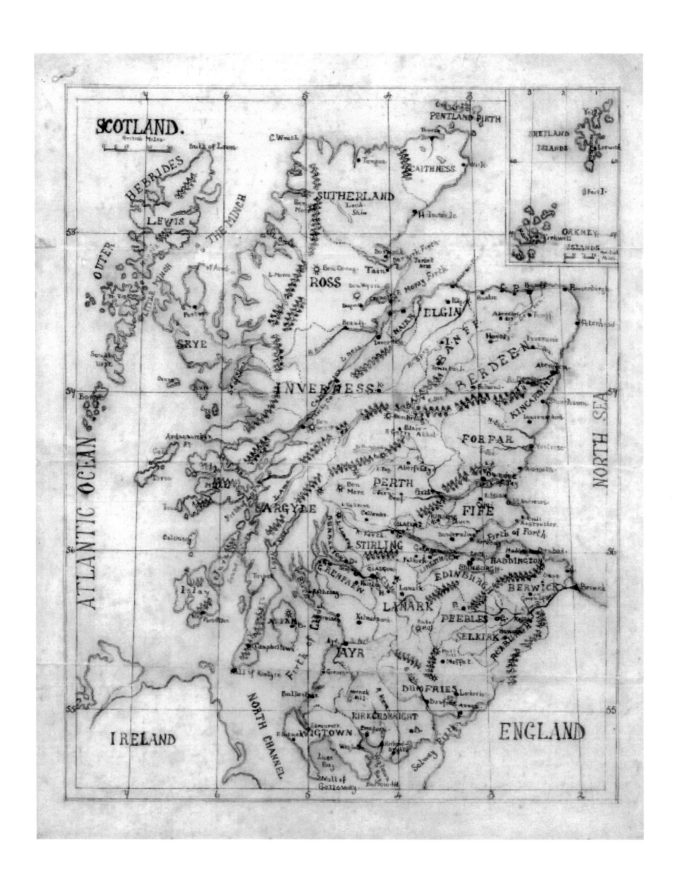

Watercolour map of Scotland by Miss Annie Alexander aged 14, which won first prize at the Portlethen Show in 1910.

order of the day – coconut shies, swingboats and sporting contests. On the same day, the village hall housed a splendid display of arts, handicrafts, horticulture and culinary skills. The hand-made, home-made subjects of competition were wide and variable: jam, honey, quilts, knitwear, cushions and rugs, embroidered tablecloths, leather goods, toys, wood-turning and painting. For instance, a watercolour map of Scotland won a first prize for my mother, Ann Alexander, aged 14 in 1910. Now resurrected and framed, this watercolour hangs in my study at home in Suffolk.

My elder sister Anne (Mrs Cormack) tells me that other relics of these events include embroidery and white work on lawn camisoles, and that Fiona, our cousin Eunice's daughter, wore one of Auntie Jessie's camisole exhibits with her going-away outfit. Anne also reminds me that one of our mother's embroidered pinafores was used to cover her wedding dress to keep it clean before her wedding day. Those items were typical of the craft entries in the hall at the Portlethen annual show. Jimmy Masson, one of Causey's grandchildren, won the "bonny baby" competition in 1938. A show of poultry and small livestock was housed in tiers of pens in the lee of the stone wall bounding the hall yard and the picnic field beyond. The many and unusual specimens on display would have gladdened the hearts of those who promote biological diversity. My repeatedly successful entry at the show was a large doe rabbit which accompanied me on summer visits to Causeyport. This pampered animal thrived on handfuls of grass and dandelions, a mash of oatmeal with used tea leaves, neeps, and bits of linseed cake intended for cattle feed.

Population changes

Following the introduction of steam trawlers in 1882, many folk in Scottish coastal villages migrated to tenements in the Torry district of Aberdeen south of the mouth of the River Dee. Similarly, many of the farming community also converged on Aberdeen for employment. The local population's international awareness was apparent in the harbour trade and in the shipyards of Lewis and of Hall Russell. Hall's shipyard built a series of famous clippers (*Thermopylae*, for example) for the China run, before Hall teamed with Russell to build steamships. Considerable numbers found it necessary to emigrate to the USA and to the countries which now comprise the Commonwealth. Before 1970, emigration caused the actual increase in the population of the general area to remain less than the natural increase. From the 1970s, the exploitation of the oil discovered off the Scottish coast resulted in a local increase in opportunities for employment. The villages surrounding Aberdeen became dormitories for commuters. The population of Portlethen increased, and its railway station, which had been closed for about thirty years, eventually reappeared on the timetables as an occasional stop for main-line passenger trains.

Portlethen Kirk stands on a prominent site, easily visible from the Aberdeen-to-Stonehaven railway line and from the main road. Using this elevated vantage point, it is possible to pick out the older buildings which have survived the changes. The earlier landmarks were the village hall, smiddie, vricht's workshop, oatmeal mill and doctor's house. The local personalities and their occupations were fewer and more easily defined than those of the present more anonymous commuters. Newer industrial developments include a meat factory and a large supermarket.

My grandfather was born at Mill of Findon, my grandmother at Mains of Findon. They started married life at the Mill before moving to Causeyport.

Alexanders at Mill of Findon

The Mill of Findon, Portlethen, was an oatmeal mill driven by a water source that suffered in two ways after the LNER railway embankment was built immediately upstream. The head of water was slower to recover, and the force of the wind which dried the corn was reduced and more fuel was required. My mother Ann, who was born at the mill in 1895, saw her birthplace fall derelict during her ninety-year lifetime. Her burial place of Portlethen kirkyard looks down on it, but she did not live to witness the restoration of the mill and the conversion of the steading to houses. Dr Clark now lives in what was the mill, and much of the nearby farmland has been built upon. What remains of the mill's seventy acres of farmland is now used by a local farmer as grazing.

A continuous succession of Alexander millers of Findon were my great-great-grandfather James, known as "Auld Elshinor" (1770–1849), his son, my great-grandfather John ("Miller Johnnie", 1809–88), and his son, my grandfather George (1853–1946), who moved from the mill to farm Causeyport in 1904 and was latterly known as "Auld Causey" (see Chapter 12). A centuries-old popular myth in North-East Scotland concerns the ploughboy who found a crock of gold which he used to start out as a farmer and/or miller. Auld Causey used to tell a version of this story concerning his own grandfather, Auld Elshinor, who moved from Bourtie parish (near Oldmeldrum) to the Portlethen area, where he married in 1803 and became the miller of Findon.

Valuation records dated November 1899 and May 1905 were kindly provided by our cousin John Alexander, a retired farmer now living in Portlethen. At that time, the Mill of Findon had one phaeton, six carts, six horse, twenty cattle and six pigs. A wide range of appropriate implements supported mixed arable farming and milling. Together with estimates for crops and muck, the total assets of George Alexander amounted to £1,316 before the move to Causeyport. This can be contrasted with the inventory of his estate upon his death forty-two years later – £22,793.

Causey's children and grandchildren heard differing versions of his stories of his ancestors. My sister Isobel recalls various tales our mother told her of growing up and of life on the farm. Auld Causey spoke of how his elder brother James (1844–87) had taken him aside before emigrating to Australia and advised him not to follow in his footsteps but to remain in Scotland with his parents. Our cousin John tells that Causey's father (also John) was reputedly a very good meal miller but turned to smuggling Dutch gin and lost a lot of money, so that as a young man Causey had to build the business up again. It did not help that James, his only brother who survived infancy, often wrote home from Australia for money, which Causey reluctantly had to send him at their father's bidding.

Their eldest sister Mary (1842–92) left for Australia shortly after James, travelling as a companion to an older lady, who unfortunately died on the journey. Mary arrived in the New World on her own, which must have been a daunting experience in those days. In a country where the men were more numerous than the women, she would have been in demand, and indeed in 1867 she married George McLennan, also a Scottish émigré, with whom she had seven children. Before they moved north to Townsville, they lived at Findon Cottage, Brisbane.

My mother had an early recollection of two incidents at the mill. She and her next younger sister, Maggie, decided to dook in the mill pond to cool off on a scorching summer's day. A primsie passenger in the train from Aberdeen chanced to spot the two nude bathers and reported this at Portlethen Station. The local postman overheard the complaint and hurried to tell the parents about their little children bathing in the pond. The other incident at the mill was when Maggie's hair got caught in moving machinery and she was forcibly turned round. Her father rushed to stop the machine, shouting "Hing in, lassie, hing in". The child was saved. Ann and baby brother John saw the incident. No doubt the three bairns were playing out of bounds.

Ritchies at Mains of Findon

The land at Mill of Findon was adjacent to the 100 acres of Mains of Findon, the home of a respected family called Ritchie. A prominent gravestone at Portlethen Kirk provides a deal of information about the Ritchies. William Alexander Ritchie (1848–1917) worked at Cookston Farm, married the farmer's daughter, Ann Carr (1851–1915), and went on to farm the Mains of

Findon. They had eight children, with roughly three-year gaps – four daughters and four sons. Their first-born was my grandmother, Mrs Ann Paterson Alexander (1872–1961). I was always intrigued by snippets of information I heard about two of my great-uncles, Bill and John, who found careers in the public service. They were portrayed as tall, clever and successful. William Alexander Ritchie (Jr), called Bill (1879–1947), was born at Cookston, the third child, and John Carr Ritchie (1885–1981), the fifth child, was the last of that family to be born at Cookston. Bill was the tallest brother, at 6' 4". At the time of his marriage to Lizzie Parry in 1908 in Holyhead, Anglesey, he was an Inland Revenue Officer. By 1910, he was a Customs and Excise Officer. He retired about 1933 at Holyhead, where he appears to have served most of his career. He directed the Excise in a region of the country from Holyhead; but his younger brother John did better. John reached the grade of Assistant Secretary in the Whitehall corridors of power – a rank which may sound humble but is greatly esteemed in the Civil Service.

I never met Bill, but I had the good fortune to meet John in the mid-1970s in Grimsby. I made annual visits to Grimsby in the late 1960s and the 1970s, to join research vessels as naturalist-in-charge of cruises to the Arctic, during the so-called "cod war". My mother prompted me to find my great-uncle and great-aunt, and an opportunity arrived while waiting for the tide. Their home at 19 Stephen Crescent, Laceby Road, was a pleasant bungalow with a flower garden, backing on to a cricket ground. The first time I called there, a dog barked at this unexpected visitor. Before John appeared from his garden, I heard him chastise his dog in the vernacular: "Haud yer whisht". Clearly, I had found the right person. Over tea, John recalled the birth of my mother Ann, the first-born to his eldest sister, also Ann, at the Mill of Findon. I invited my great-uncle John and his wife (also Ann!) to meet the captain and the somewhat inebriated crew aboard the research vessel *Cirolana* before sailing time.

I was able to confirm the following facts, having heard stories about the scholarship and careers of the two brothers, particularly John. He attended Robert Gordon's College and was class dux. He then attended Burnett's School, Golden Square, Aberdeen. Mr Burnett prepared candidates for the Civil Service "Boy Clerk's Competition". John achieved first place in the kingdom in this open competition. Mr Burnett quoted John's success to advertise his school, and actually paid John to remain as his star pupil and sit further competitive examinations. John agreed to enrol, provided he could study by correspondence from home at the Mains of Findon. It was all the same to Mr Burnett. His courses were sent and returned by train. In due course, John's academic achievements entitled him to start off at a decent grade in the Civil Service.

John is not mentioned on the Portlethen stone, but Ivor has traced his marriage records. Bachelor John, on his 24th birthday in 1909, married Ada M. C. C. J. S. Hendry, 19-year-old daughter of a Supervisor of Inland Revenue, in York where she lived (though born in Dunkeld). Widower John, aged 53, was married in 1938 to Ann M. Feeney, aged 29, spinster, an Irish Catholic lady. My mother told me that when someone expressed surprise at his plans to marry a Roman Catholic, John replied: "I would marry Ann if she were a Moslem". John told me that he had retired to Dublin and lived there for twenty-five years on a good pension, paying less tax than he would have been required to pay if resident in the UK. They returned in 1964 to Grimsby, where John died in 1981 aged 96, survived by Ann.

My grandmother's youngest brother, Alexander George (Sanny) Ritchie, was born only a few months before our mother. When he came to visit and play with his nieces and nephews, he was always called Uncle Sandy, much to the amusement of the men on the farm. As the only son who grew up and stayed in Scotland, he took over the Mains of Findon lease following his father.

2

Move to Causeyport

Young family

At Martinmas (November) 1904, the present Causeyport farmhouse was completed and the Alexander family moved there from the Mill of Findon. My grandparents, George Alexander (Auld Causey, 1853–1946) and Ann Paterson Ritchie (1872–1961), lived at Causeyport Farm from 1904 to 1943. According to Auld Causey, the previous tenant was insolvent. As my sister Isobel notes, money must have been pretty tight about that time, as our mother recalled that sovereigns given to the children as presents from Grandfather Ritchie "disappeared" around then.

Five of the seven Alexander children were born at Mill of Findon: Ann (1895), Margaret (1897), John (1899), Jessie (1902) and Mary (1904), who was six months of age at the time of the move. Dod (1906) and Mina (1910) were born at Causeyport, completing this family.

Four sisters celebrating Easter 1908. Back, left to right: Ann Paterson Alexander, Margaret Hay Alexander. Front, left to right: Mary Jane Alexander, Jessie Brechin Alexander.

Stony ground

Causeyport is a mixed arable and dairy farm of 204 acres about five miles south of Aberdeen. It is situated between the Banchory-Devenick crossroads and the stone circle at Craighead. The farm's name may suggest an entrance, gate or causeway. Striated stones, of diverse geological origin, are evident in the surrounding soil, apparently transported during glaciation. During the agrarian revolution, the larger stones were cleared from the land and skilfully manhandled to construct the dry-stane dykes, which are now permanent walls delimiting fields and roads. These walls are a distinctive feature of the arable landscape of north-east Scotland. Rough stones were used to "foun the rucks" in the Causeyport corn yard. One particularly prominent stone stood in the centre of the Langstane park, one of the Causeyport fields to the left of the road going south from the farm. It is probable that this feature related to the several prehistoric circles of standing stones in the surrounding area, such as the Craighead "Druid" Circle on the high ground past the road junction to the south of Causeyport. Beasts may have used this langstane as a scratching post for some five millennia. Sadly, some irreverent vandal considered this langstane an impediment to modern cultivation and removed it some time after Auld Causey's roup in 1943.

3

Transport

Governor's car

The early means of transport for the farmer and his family at Causeyport was a horse-drawn governor's car, but, by the time I started to take notice, there was no shelt to pull this elegant vehicle, which was stored in a long black shed, opening on to the close, opposite the cart shed. My father remembered seeing my mother at the reins driving this vehicle. Causey would take his young family in it for a picnic outing as far as Dunnottar.

Lights of Aberdeen

I recall being a passenger in my father's Rover 14 car, approaching Aberdeen from the south before the 1939 "blackout". It was fun to see the brilliantly lit city vanish and reappear between each twist and turn of the downhill "cart-track" approach to the Auld Bridge of Dee. From that distance, some of Aberdeen's cinemas could be identified by their new neon lights. The neon light then above Rossleigh Garage, Forbesfield Road, illuminated the back of our home at Burns Road. It outshone the coal-gas-mantle lantern in the back lane lit by the leerie with his pole and wick. I remember the amused reaction of two sophisticated daughters of my great-aunt Peg Park (Margaret Ritchie), on a visit home from Washington DC, USA, on seeing our leerie in action. What could they have thought about young children going to bed carrying candles in the Causeyport farmhouse?

Bus

During the 1940s, the bus serving Causeyport was an Alexander's "Bluebird", from its terminus in Dee Street, Aberdeen, to Stonehaven and beyond. Its route crossed the Auld Bridge of Dee, then followed the Aberdeen-to-Stonehaven "turnpike" road. The way south, up from the bridge, was a winding, uphill journey, a tiresome drag on a pedal cycle, or for a cart horse anxious to get home. (The present bus route crosses the recent bridge and follows the now transformed dual carriageway, renumbered "A90".) The bus stop adjacent to Causeyport was at Findon School, a good mile east of the farm. Looking from Findon School, the distant Causeyport steading appeared as a clump of mature deciduous trees. An unmade but flat and straight cart track, called the "auld road", stretched from opposite Findon Schoolhouse to the Causeyport cottar houses. To the north of this track lay a peat moss with its white tufts of bog-cotton, midges, dragonflies and nests of emmerteens under loose stones. On summer holidays from school, these Causeyport children herded cattle grazing on the moss. The children ran barefoot in summer and found it uncomfortable to push their hardened feet back into boots to walk to school. By contrast, most modern children get fashionable trainers and a car-ride to school.

Tollahill

An alternative route from Aberdeen to Causeyport by car or bicycle, or on foot, was as follows. Cross the Auld Bridge of Dee, and turn west along the South Deeside Road towards Blairs, then turn south up Tollahill at the sign "Causeyport Road", past Banchory-Devenick school and through the crossroads where stood the smiddie. I recall taking implements for repair in a box cart to this blacksmith, Willie Clark. I associate the smiddie with clanging metal, flying sparks and the unmistakable odour of singeing hoof. I have vivid memories of the smith forging and fitting horseshoes. He would crank the shaft of the bellows with one hand, making the forge roar. His other hand would grasp a long pair of tongs holding a piece of incandescent metal, which he proceeded to hammer into shape on the anvil. The smith crouched under the horse, holding a hoof firmly between his knees, through an open gusset in his leather apron. Each singeing hot shoe was fitted against its hoof. The smith then pared down the scorched areas on the hoof to make the shoe fit snugly, before securing it with nails. Each hoof was smoothed off using a rasp and given a brush of oil. My Uncle Dod thought that Willie Clark had a good way with the young horses, which were shod at Banchory-Devenick. The workhorses were shod at the Portlethen smiddie, which stood at another crossroads, on what was then the main Aberdeen-to-Stonehaven road.

Opposite the Banchory-Devenick smiddie stood a wee shop with a clanging bell attached to the door and a candlestick telephone for public use. The standard cost of a telephone call was two old pence (2d = 0.83p in decimal coinage). I had neither cause nor coppers to use this fascinating instrument. Occasionally, my grandfather sent me there to fetch him an ounce of Erinmore pipe tobacco, which cost 8d in the old coinage (3.33p). From the Banchory-Devenick crossroads, proceed down the hill past the stone quarry, and Causeyport is the second farm steading on the right. (My sister Anne reminds me that her wee brother got stuck while climbing the stone wall of the quarry.) Walking from Aberdeen to Causeyport was enough to build up a thirst for fresh milk and an appetite for oatcakes (quarters of breid), crumbly blue cheese and buttered scones, all home-made by my venerable granny.

Market day

In the late 1930s and into the 1940s, George Alexander (Auld Causey) travelled regularly by Morris car to and from Aberdeen on Friday market days. His son George (Dod Causey) told me that his father never learned to drive, but registered and insured the car in his own name and simply handed the same documents to his son and namesake, who did all the driving. While Causey went about his market business, Dod collected and transported the weekly provisions from Scorgie the grocer in Rose Street and Spence Alsop the butcher in the New Market by the Green. The butcher's wooden floor had a daily covering of fresh sawdust to absorb any blood or siclike.

4

Layout of house and steading

Close and yard

The enclosed areas between the farm buildings are collectively called the close. To describe Causeyport, it is convenient to distinguish a straight close at right angles to the road, and an enclosed yard on to which most of the steading doors opened. The back and west sides of the house met the yard.

South of the house

The garden was to the front (south) and road side (east) of the house. The area in front of the house was laid out in an (Italianate) geometrical pattern of paths and beds defined by low, square-trimmed box hedging. I cannot imagine that Causey himself would have had the patience to lay out such a design. Perhaps the daughters of the household were responsible. To the south of the front garden, a high privet hedge concealed the cattle lane which ran from the road to the two long byres. To the south of the lane was an enclosed ree, containing a flock of laying hens, then the midden opposite the two doors on the south gables of the stirks' byre and the milking byre. The privy was semi-detached to the double byre, behind a patch of very productive blackcurrant bushes, which were heavy with berries when grandchildren visited during summer holidays. To this day, our cousin Eunice cannot smell blackcurrants without remembering that corner of the garden.

East of the house

The area between the east side of the house and the road was in grass, with large trees along the roadside. A stone cheese press (see page 22 for photograph) stood in the area of grass between the dairy and the road. A wooden platform at the roadside supported milk cans for daily collection. The drying green was between the road and the black shed parallel to the road.

West of the house

The west side of the house looked across the yard past the peat stack at a doocot on the gable by the door to the byres. In clockwise direction from the house, the yard gave access to a short double byre at right angles to the stirks' byre. The dairy byre was parallel to and beyond the stirks' byre. The straw shed was between the stirks' byre and the mill, which was within the north-west corner of the buildings limiting the yard.

North of the house

The close at right angles to the main road led up to the corn yard. On the right of this close, in order from the road, was a parking space for implements in front of a field gate, the cart shed, stables, a rather arbitrary building which held piglets or colts at different times, and the bothy. The open-fronted cart shed housed a four-wheeled wagon painted blue, and six brightly painted, red and green box carts. Their paired wooden spoked wheels had steel rims, about five foot in diameter.

The stable block was free-standing. The main stable had six stalls for working horses, and the adjoining lesser stable had two stalls, with travises and mangers of stout wooden construction. The floor was cobbled. The high door to the hayloft was above the main stable door. Hay was passed through a hatch at the end of the loft straight down a wooden chute and collected in the stable after lifting a vertically sliding wooden sash. The wooden stair to the loft was at the other end. The corn kist under a window contained bruised oats, dispensed in a square box. The stable door and horse trough faced the yard, and looked towards the back door of the house. The stable midden was to the north behind the stables. My sister Isobel recalls that playing in the hayloft above the stable was a great source of entertainment, as was the rope swing strung over the rafters in the stirks' byre (the stirks were out on pasture for the summer). The great feat was to swing high enough to touch the cobwebbed rafters with your toes.

The south side of the close, that is on the left starting from the road, was the drying green, black shed. (The innermost recesses of the long black shed contained the governor's car and enough obsolete farm implements and artefacts to furnish a rural museum.) Next was the coalhouse gable and the entrance to the main yard. Past the yard opening stood the wing with the stone steps on its east gable and the threshing mill in its far end. The steps to the loft door had no hand rail. This wing of the steading housed the mill, a loose box with the usual half-door, and a workshop, in which paraffin was stored. The loft above had a west door giving raised access so that sheaves of corn could be delivered, from a cart, to the top of the mill.

The dairy was in one end of a building stretching from near the back door of the house to the close. The dairy door faced a scullery window. It was more convenient to the house than to the byre. Sections of the same building contiguous with the dairy, under one continuous roof, housed young turkeys and hens, also coal and firewood. The poultry had the freedom of the yard, even up to the back door.

Plan of Causeyport Farm house and steading, not to scale
(Two cottar houses are outwith this area)

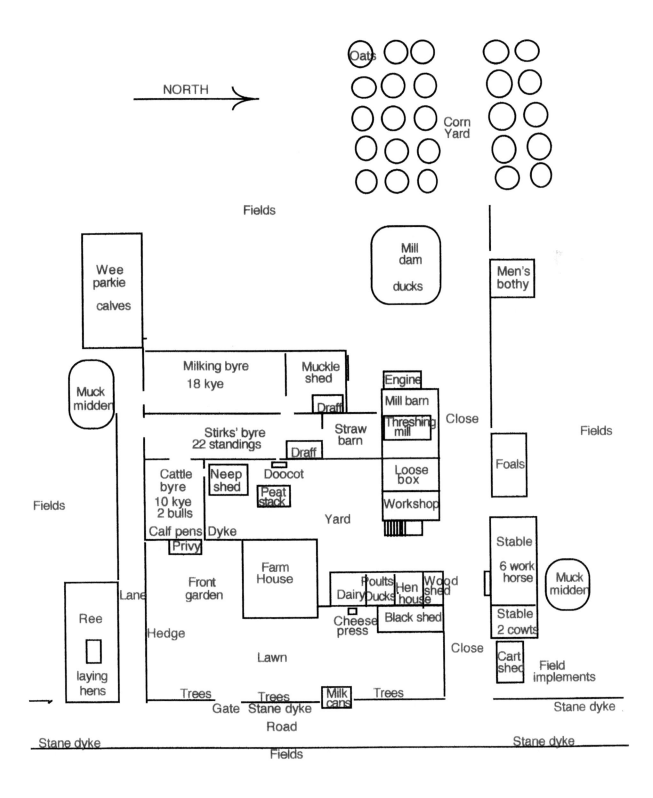

NORTH

Oats

Corn
Yard

Fields

Mill
dam

ducks

Men's
bothy

Wee
parkie

calves

Muck
midden

Milking byre
18 kye

Muckle
shed

Draff

Engine

Mill barn

Threshing
mill

Close

Fields

Straw
barn

Stirks' byre
22 standings

Draff

Loose
box

Foals

Fields

Cattle
byre
10 kye
2 bulls

Neep
shed

Doocot

Peat
stack

Workshop

Yard

Calf pens Dyke

Privy

Stable
6 work
horse

Muck
midden

Front
garden

Farm
House

Poults
Dairy Ducks

Hen
house

Wood
shed

Lane

Black shed

Stable
2 cowts

Ree

Hedge

Cheese
press

Close

Cart
shed

Field
implements

laying
hens

Lawn

Trees

Trees

Milk
cans

Trees

Gate Stane dyke

Stane dyke

Road

Stane dyke

Stane dyke

Fields

11

5

House plan

Interior

The Causeyport farmhouse was reconstructed before the Alexander family moved in, hence the date 1904 engraved in the grey granite above the front door. This house had about ten rooms. The family quarters were in the main south front of the house facing the flower garden. Downstairs, at the front, there was a sitting-room/dining-room, a vestibule, hall and a drawing-room/parlour, or music room. The choice of names for rooms depends on their uses and on the pretensions of the users. The family Bible was kept there together with some ancient papers concerning the Mill of Findon. My sister Anne says that one of these mementos was defaced by a childish hand writing "Hairy Mary Jane". Of course, I was far too young to admit any guilt. Granny tried to dissuade us grandchildren from using the drawing-room as a romper room. We wanted to use the upholstered, round pouffe as a vehicle, and were fascinated by a smooth, cylindrical, polished granite artefact about four inches in diameter, a granite-industry by-product that was used as a hearth ornament.

A handsome stairway led from the central hall to an upstairs landing. A single bedroom at ground level faced the yard; fresh eggs were stored in the cold bathroom opposite, which had a long, galvanised tin bath and a window facing towards the road. A press below the stairs was used to store bread, square tins of biscuits, and groceries. Upstairs were four large bedrooms, with a boxroom above the front hall. The bedrooms had brass bedsteads, horsehair or feather mattresses, woollen blankets, feather quilts and clootie bedside rugs. The stone-top washstands had matching basin, ewer and chamber pot. Stone water bottles, called pigs, were used to heat the beds in winter. It is difficult for some English-born people to appreciate that Scottish farm folk went to bed with "pigs" while their servants lay on "caff" (chaff).

Kitchen

A central door in the main passage through the ground floor separated the family dining and living quarters in the front of the house from the back, which contained the men's kitchen and kitchen-scullery. A stair behind a plain door in the men's kitchen led up to the deem's room. "Kitchie deem" is a local term for an unmarried kitchen maid living in part of the farmhouse. This room was seldom occupied at Causeyport. Just inside the kitchen door and up on the wall, a system of swinging bells were each identified with different living areas in the front of the house, wherein the bells were operated by small levers set into the walls. This kitchen had a large girnel containing a copious supply of oatmeal, and a pine dresser holding striped bowls and plates. The pine table and matching chairs had sturdy square legs. The stone floor withstood tacketie boots. An old sepia-tone photograph on the kitchen wall showed William Ritchie, Causey's father-in-law, leading a Shorthorn cow. Perhaps the cow was "Yalder", the subject of one of William Ritchie's repertoire of surviving poems and writings now collected and printed in booklet form.

Range

In the same room where the men ate, the black-leaded range had all the equipment for cooking meals and baking oatcakes, scones, pancakes and the like. Peat was the preferred fuel. The range had an oven on one side and a water tank on the other, also a swye and swingle on which to hang and manoeuvre the black cast-iron kettle, pot and girdle. Gloves were worn to clean, scour, brush and polish the range, using emery paper and "Zebo" black-lead paste to prevent oxidation.

6

Services

Water

A dam above the steading and opposite the bothy had once supplied a mill lade running alongside the close and powering a water-wheel. By the 1930s, the dam was a duck pond; the mill lade was enclosed and the water-wheel gone. I assume that the water came from a natural well somewhere to the west of Causeyport. Plumbing was minimal: water was piped to the scullery sink, the horse trough outside the stable, the cooler in the dairy, the milking byre and the bothy. In the kitchen, two large wooden tubs stood under the east window next to a huge boiler encased in stone and cement with a live fire below and a chimney in the corner of the back wall. Cats liked the boiler fire and came so close to the falling hot ashes that their fur got singed. Hot water, as required, was not piped but lifted out using a hemispherical metal scoop with a short wooden handle.

The household bath had no piped supply. It was hung on a wall hook in the next room and was seldom used. There was no water supply to the privy – a stone building, a respectful distance out from the front of the house, in a corner of the garden adjoining the wall of the double byre. The privy's external wall was thickly enveloped in dark green ivy which almost concealed the door. Although flush mechanisms date from roughly 1880, there was no flush lavatory at Causeyport, only a dry two-holer, one larger one smaller, with a supply of cut newspaper on a nail – no tap, hand-basin, soap or towel. A bucket of water, soft soap and a scrubbing brush freshened up the white wooden bench seat, which was hinged so that pails could be lifted out and carried through a slap in the privet hedge and the soil emptied on the byre midden. The men relieved themselves directly on the midden or on the land. The brown water in the open drain or burn which ran alongside the auld road by the two cottar houses was aptly named the "strang burn". Despite primitive facilities, the folk at Causeyport enjoyed rude health and considerable longevity.

Fuel

An oil engine replaced the water-wheel as a source of power. The piston of this diesel engine turned a big flywheel. Its speed was regulated by a pair of spinning ball governors. This engine was housed in a black wooden lean-to shed, outside the wall to the west of the mill. Another machine in this shed was a large vintage motorcycle, belonging to Dod Alexander.

A mobile steam engine, which could both haul and drive a mobile mill, was introduced to thrash out the corn yard. The steam engine burned up to a ton of coal over three days.

Causeyport had no electricity – main or generator. Illumination was by portable paraffin lamps or candles. Encased lanterns were carried and hung in the farm steading. Granny did embroidery by the light of a delicately adjusted Tilley lamp which made a soft purring sound. Some of the better household lamps had mantles, others had only wicks. Peat fires heated the house and bothy. The peat was cast on the moss. Dry peat was brought home in box carts, then stacked in the yard between the kitchen window and the doocot by the byre door. An outhouse contained some coal, but Auld Causey and others preferred the homely smell of burning peat to stinking coal.

Cable

In 1940, an electric cable was laid along the public road past the end of the Causeyport close; but it served only the new radar masts, which were a crucial part of the nation's air defence system.

7

Workers

Living quarters

Family household members were actively employed on the farm, on the general assumption that all should work for their keep. The hired men were as follows: grieve, foreman, second and third horsemen, a cattle bailie and an orraman (odd-job man). The grieve and the bailie lived with their families in the two south-facing cottar houses about 100m north of the steading, at the junction with the cart track called the auld road. The single men lived in a free-standing two-room bothy, up the close, on the right, opposite the mill dam. One bothy room had a fireplace on the central wall. In the other room, three box beds had curved sides which resembled the travises in the stable, presumably made by the same craftsman. The mattresses were canvas ticking bags filled with caff from the mill. Each man in the bothy kept his personal belongings in a heavy wooden kist of local construction. My father, Samuel Jamieson, continued to keep mementos in his kist long after he had left the land.

Muckle Friday

Muckle Friday feein' market occurred on two of the Scottish quarter-days, Whitsun (May) and Martinmas (November). Fee'd men were engaged for a half-year term. Men offering themselves for hire congregated in the Castlegate, Aberdeen, as in other market towns. Each man contracted to serve a farmer for the following six months, and a shilling from the farmer sealed a verbal agreement. The same shilling is now 5p in decimal money. An agreed fee was due to the servant on completion of the half-year term. Any money he begged from the farmer in the interval was deducted from the agreed amount. The single men fed in the farm kitchen and lived in a bothy or chaumer. Meal, milk and tatties were included in kind in the transaction for cottars. They carried home a half-gallon can of freshly cooled but unpasteurised milk at the end of each day. The hired men were expected home to start work on the evening of Muckle Friday, in time to attend to the beasts, of course. So much for their biannual day of freedom! On the farms on Muckle Friday, there were no hired men to feed, and the bothy bed covers were changed for washing.

The traditional Muckle Friday ceased during the Second World War (1939–45), when labour was frozen and military conscription applied. From 1940, farm workers were valued as producers of food, essential to the war effort. Packs of German U-boats and pocket battleships, aiming to starve the British population into surrender, were sinking far too many of the food ships crossing the Atlantic. After the war, more modern employment arrangements replaced the old feudal customs.

8

Muck and magic

Crops and seasons

Causeyport's 204 acres of mixed crops and livestock were divided by dry-stane dykes requiring minimal maintenance. The crops included potatoes, oats (called "corn"), barley, turnips, hay and pasture grazed by cattle and horses. According to the demands of the particular seasons, the men toiled in Causeyport's fields, ploughing, harrowing, sowing, hoeing, mowing, reaping, forking, pickin' tatties, pu'in' neeps, casting peats, milling corn, repairing stone walls, laying clay-pipe drains in fields, herding, grooming, mucking out byres, stables and poultry houses and duly spreading the matured muck back on the land.

The outdoor work at Causeyport was cyclical and seasonal, supporting the rotation of hay and pasture with crops of neeps, oats, barley and potatoes, all at the mercy of the weather. Farming up to the 1940s used the time-honoured organic methods, now rediscovered by the trendy ecofreak minority. Ploughmen walked behind horse-drawn implements. Cows were hand-milked. The introductions of Swedish turnips and Dutch clover in the nineteenth century had improved the diet and practically eliminated the winter mortality of livestock. Rotted manure was returned to the soil. Guano, the excrement of seafowl, was available so long as the Peruvian anchovies survived the vagaries of Pacific Ocean currents to support great populations of sea birds roosting on the cliffs. This fertiliser arrived in hessian sacks, which were put to many uses about the farm. Lime was applied to counteract sour soil. Basic slag, applied to the soil, arrived in deceptively small bags, each weighing a memorable 2½ hundredweight, equivalent to 127 kilogrammes. The carrying technique was to take the weight low down on the back and keep the legs straight. I said to myself: "Never again if I can help it".

Hoeing (hyowin)

As the rain and sun encouraged the neeps to grow, small teams of men moved methodically along the drills singling the seedlings and dislodging the weeds. If the weather remained dry enough, the dislodged vegetation withered between the drills, and the singled neeps grew at six-inch intervals, that being the breadth of the hyow blade. Experienced hyowers left neat and rounded drills, while this inexperienced toonser loon struggled on the tail end of the team. As with many farm tasks, this work was repetitive; but an open field on a fine day presented a good opportunity for conversation.

Haymaking (hey)

Haymaking was fun in the sun – the zenith of my time at Causeyport. The mixture of herbage included rich blue clover and ripe rye grass. Anticipating the ripening of the hay, a group of men in the doorway of the black shed undid new hanks of reddish-brown, twisted coir. They rolled this rope into balls of a size and weight suitable for throwing over the tops of coles and haystacks. The alternative tying method used ropes of dried hay, which were made using a thraw hook (like a hand brace with a hook instead of a bit), as and when required in the field. Hay was cut by a horse-drawn mower, raked into rows by a horse-drawn rake usually driven by a youth, and stacked in coles. When suitably dried in the wind, each cole was hauled, by a tracer rope hooked to the haims on the horse's collar, to the edge of the field, where the hay was stacked in rucks.

Children rode bareback all day, dragging in the dry coles. They were safer mounted than leading. One man in the field tucked the tracer rope into the base of each cole. As each ruck got higher, the two-toed pitchforks laden with hay were passed hand to hand by men standing back on to the ladder against the ruck. Empty pitchforks were slid down by the side of the ladder, pierced the soil, and were grasped to repeat the forking routine. In building each ruck, the hay was radially layered, sloping downwards and outwards to shed the rain. Each completed ruck was tied down using ropes made on the spot using a thraw hook.

Harvest (hairst)

At Causeyport, in the 1940s, roads were scythed and sheaves hand-bound along the perimeters of ripe cornfields to make access routes for a horse-drawn reaper. The reaper continuously cut, bound and ejected the sheaves of barley or oats. Pairs of sheaves were raxed up, one in each oxter, and firmly slapped together, head to head, as they were set up in stooks. Each stook had four pairs of sheaves, set in line with the prevailing wind. The wind-dried sheaves were forked on to carts. Each cart had a heck on which to spread the load. The crop was drawn home and stacked on rough stone foundations in the corn yard, which was at the top of the close, beyond the mill dam and bothy.

Steam mill (stame mull)

A threshing mill, transported and driven by one and the same mobile steam engine, was hired for about two days to thresh the corn stacked in the yard. A continuous belt connected the fly-wheel of the engine with the drive-wheel of the mill. All the stacks of sheaves in the corn yard were reduced to sacks of corn, stacks of straw and mounds of chaff. Casual workers hired for this intensive activity were well fed in the farm kitchen. A very large black pot was required for the broth. In the middle of each half-day yoking, each worker got a bottle of Bass to clear the stour from his throat. This youth helped to rake out chaff from below the mill and earned his ale along with the rest. He acquired a taste for the produce of Burton-on-Trent.

Tatties, neeps, peats and muck

The potato harvest was labour-intensive, and local schoolchildren were given "tattie holidays" to meet this need. The town schools did not close for tattie holidays, but I would have preferred the fields to the classroom. The tatties were stored in the field in long pits covered in straw, then soil. To feed the cattle in winter, neeps were manually pulled from the soil and transported home in box carts – an unpleasant task in rain and mud, but Clydesdale hooves, with the dimensions of dinner-plates, are well adapted to cope with a depth of mud approaching the cart axles. Pu'in' neeps was even more daunting in frozen soil. It was imperative that the animals be fed. Most of the tasks relied on physical strength. Milking by hand is a strenuous activity. Forking out the muck middens and casting peats were reputedly the most physically demanding tasks. I am so glad I did not have to endure either.

Iron horse

A Fordson tractor arrived about 1939. It had iron wheels treaded with iron spikes, no rubber tyres and no cabin to protect the driver from the elements. The iron seat had no cushion. It was metal with holes in it like the seat on most horse-drawn farm implements, and sprung on a strap of steel.

On rough ground, this teenage driver was bounced uncomfortably, maintaining contact with the vehicle by clinging firmly to the steering wheel. The engine was initially fuelled by petrol, while it was manually cranked to start. As soon as the engine got running, a tap on the Y-shaped fuel line was switched to paraffin for normal running. Some implements, which had been horse-drawn previously, were modified for attachment to this new tractor.

Implements

At Causeyport, I learned to marvel at the ingenuity of design in some of the simple implements and at the associated skills, which had more in common with the distant past than with current technology. The design of the scythe must have been a great advance over the sickle. The binder-tow-tying mechanism was a most remarkable invention, sparing much backbreaking work. As the mower and binder superseded the scythe, the combine harvester superseded the reaper and the steam mill. The once universal pitchfork is now insignificant. What about the products of coopers, wheelwrights and saddlers – the barrel, cartwheel, wheelbarrow, yoke, horse collar and harness? Consider, for example, the highly evolved construction of the box cart with its adjustable shelvings, back door, heck and skilfully constructed wheels. A suitably harnessed and yoked horse could haul a balanced one-ton load through glaur or mire. The box-cart load could be emptied quickly. The balanced relationship of the shaft pins and the wheel axle is such that when the pin holding the box to the shafts is removed, and the horse moves back, the load is tipped. As the horse moves forward, the box is recovered and secured to the shafts by replacing the pin. The kind cooperation of worker and beast is taken for granted.

In the city of Aberdeen, where the roads were set in granite causeys, heavy horses hauled four-wheeled flat lorries to transport heavy goods from the docks and to distribute the sacks of coal often carried up tenement stairs. Steel sharps were set into horseshoes during snow and ice. A tracer was yoked in tandem to assist heavy loads up Market Street. Scaffie cairts had pull-down canvas covers to shield the refuse against the wind. Bakers' horse-drawn vans were designed to enclose trays of bread, cakes and rowies, while other vans were designed to carry milk, groceries and so on. The drivers on rounds used street cries. The grain that spilled from horses' nosebags supported doos and spugs. An arbitrary assortment of horses and vehicles distributed boxes of fish from the trawler dock. The smell of fish confronted visitors arriving at the LNER terminal in the Joint Station, where a fleet of early Rolls Royce taxis welcomed returning exiles and astonished newcomers expecting to find London-style cabs.

More sweat

Causey's horse-drawn generation and earlier generations used the labour-intensive, sweat-and-toil methods which are now replaced by mechanisation and bulk transport. Milk was handled in pails and transported in ten-gallon cans (73.8 litres). The normal packaging of potatoes, grain and fertiliser was coarse hessian bags. The standard sack of potatoes weighed 112 lb, or one hundred-weight ("1 cwt" is 50.8 kg). Each quarter of oats weighed 3 cwt, whereas a quarter of barley weighed 4 cwt. Cotton bags of wheat flour imported from North America weighed a manageable 120 lb, which is 54.4 kg.

9

Food

Brose

The men's breakfast was brose – the ingredients oatmeal, salt, boiling water and cream. A bowl of natural milk was set at each place on the pine table the previous evening. This allowed the cream to rise. A plate covered each bowl to deter any cat, mouse or insect. The large wooden girnel held an abundant supply of oatmeal. The meal and salt were measured into an empty bowl from the dresser.

Each man helped himself to roughly four, or even up to six, spoonfuls of oatmeal, according to appetite and digestive capacity. Add a big pinch of salt to savour the splendid flavour of the oat. A slurp of boiling water was added, from the black kettle swinging on the range, and immediately mixed to form a thick paste. The consistency of brose is such that only the handle end of the spoon is capable of mixing it efficiently. The bowl was immediately covered with a side plate and left to stand for a minute to allow the mixture to swell. Add the top of the milk from the other bowl, lick clean the spoon handle, and get supping. Figuratively speaking, brose sticks to the ribs. As this concentrated food continues to swell after it is consumed, it is suitable only for people who are totally committed to sustained physical activity throughout the following yoking. A hired man would walk up to twenty miles on the land behind a pair of horse in a ten-hour day, six days a week. Brose was the sustenance of drovers herding beef cattle to Smithfield, and of soldiers on forced marches. Brose was the diet of those who cleared the land of stones and whins and the dry-stane dykers who changed the face of the countryside between about 1750 and 1850. Custom makes a virtue out of this necessity. In reality, a craving for brose is readily acquired and much relished in harsh and demanding circumstances.

Curiously, brose was not restricted to breakfast. Varieties of oatmeal brose were made using the boiling bree from boiled kale or neeps. Similarly, porridge was not restricted to breakfast but occasionally served for supper, when it tastes quite different for no apparent reason. Incidentally, accepted custom refers to broth and brose as "they" – a plural I find hard to justify. Admittedly, the constituents of broth are many; but brose should not be lumpy.

Tatties

Tattie time was at "hal twal" (11:30am), the logical half of the twelfth hour. The fee'd men, in galluses, belts and nickie-tams, would swipe the muck from their tacketie boots with the stable brush, flick the stour from their dungers with a horse dandy, and showd ben the yard from the stable to the farm kitchen in order of seniority: foreman, second, third, orraman and loon. (Dungarees were called "dungers" and were made of blue denim, *serge de Nîmes*, originally from Nîmes in France. Some farm servants wore smart lightweight denim jackets, called clean land jackets, which were of a more conventional cut than the more modern "battledress" style.)

Tatties and oatmeal were the mainstay ingredients of the main meal at midday. The food was plain and wholesome. Of course, there was no choice or à la carte. The traditional soups were Scotch vegetable broth, lentil soup, tattie soup and leek soup. The main course was never beefsteak and chips, neither mixed grill nor burger, but more probably beef mince and tatties. Other favourites were stovies (étouffée), mutton pies, Forfar bridies, mealie puddings, and herring either rolled and soused in vinegar or dabbed in oatmeal then fried. Fried patties were made from reconstituted dried cod, potatoes and mustard. The men called this "hairy tatties". Oatmeal skirlie was used to eke out the meat. I must not forget clootie dumplings (cooked in broth), or custard, or yirned milk (curds). The main vegetables were the obligatory tatties, neeps, carrots, cabbage and kale. Pickled sliced beetroot was the popular garnish. After eating, it was usual for the men to doze off among the hay while the horses fed and rested before yoking again at one o'clock. The working routine was governed largely by the horses' need to feed, drink and rest. Tea breaks were not an established part of the working routine, but tea was brought out to the fields at the height of the hay and harvest seasons. A chanced "fly cup" was never an excuse to linger. The supper meal at 6pm could be boiled eggs or cheese and breid (oatcakes) or fish, and plain loaf, scones or pancakes, with butter, syrup or jam. Fruit was uncommon, except in home-made jams and jellies made from wild rasps, brambles or blaeberries. Syrup was a common substitute for jam, particularly on pancakes or scones. Beverages were tea, or water; no fruit juice or soft drink. Crates of bottled Bass appeared exceptionally when the steam mill was in action.

Fish

A triangular wooden heck hung on the outside gable of the dairy, near the back door, supporting fish on nails. Fish were bought at the back door from the wicker creel carried on the back of the fishwife trudging miles from the shore.

Diet, health and surgery

I frequently enjoyed the fare as described above. This diet was appropriate for labourers toiling in a cool climate. Habits die hard, and mothers' food is always considered to be the best, but the above diet is not compatible with modern sedentary living. Only the lucky few now get the benefit of heart surgery.

10

Animals

Horses

Three pairs of Clydesdale horse were used to work the land at Causeyport. The foreman, second horseman and third horseman had a pair each. I remember the individual animals. Donald the gelding and Meg were chestnut, Tib was dun, Bess was black and Onar was a strawberry roan mare. The horses were related within a common female lineage, in that they were replaced from stock born of Causeyport mares, all reared and broken to harness at Causeyport. The sires of the foals were magnificently groomed Clydesdale stallions which proudly walked the countryside, each led by his groom. A pair of foals was born annually and reared on the farm, giving a contemporary total of up to twelve horse, including working horse, breeding mares, cowts, fillies and foals. My Uncle Dod was enthusiastically interested in the developing young horses.

The Clydesdale breed reached its greatest popularity in the 1920s, then declined in numbers, escaped extinction in the 1960s and has now recovered to a minimal sustainable level. Teams of Clydesdales remain popular for pulling drays advertising breweries in the UK and the USA.

Cattle

The three herds at Causeyport were a hand-milked herd of about twenty Dairy Shorthorn cattle, a herd of Shorthorns suckling crossbred calves, and a herd of home-bred black stirks and heifers – and two black Aberdeen Angus bulls, one older and one younger. One bull served the dairy herd while the other served the kye which were suckling black calves. The Shorthorn coos were red, roan, or red with some white. The calves were out of Dairy Shorthorn cows mated to Aberdeen Angus bulls, hence the hummel black calves and stirks expressing two dominant paternal genes, one for naturally polled heads and the other for uniformly black coats. The black stirks had the short, dumpy, fat characteristics of "baby beef", which was highly popular. The youngest calves were kept in pens in the byre, and others in the wee parkie near the byre door. They drank milk from hand-held buckets, and the stronger calves became boisterous, boxing at their buckets.

A neighbour's black bull once got through a boundary and challenged one of Causeyport's bulls. The two hornless beasts, each weighing about a ton, were spinning with surprising agility and butting one another. When I told Dod, he immediately grasped two forks and handed me one of them. Dod's advice was: "Dinna be feart tae ram it hame. Their hide is as thick as the sole o' yer boot, so you winna penetrate." We parted the two beasts, but it seemed that my heart was pumping in my throat. Dod joked about picadors, but I did not feel like singing the "Toreador Song" from *Carmen*. Isobel recalls me once sitting on the back of one of the cows which she was helping to bring to the byre for milking, with an agitated bull nearby. Uncle Dod was thought very brave and clever sitting on a bull's back and sliding over its head, but the Aberdeen Angus bulls at Causeyport were more docile than the Ayrshire bulls at Glithno in later years.

At the mart

I recall Causey purchasing an Irish-bred Shorthorn cow at the Kittybrewster mart. Causey had his own ideas and prejudices about the anatomy of a good dairy cow. He inspected everything from the veins along the beast's belly to the length of its tail. After much handling, back-scratching and condemnation of the extortionate asking price, a deal was agreed and the cow joined the dairy herd at Causeyport. Dod was suspicious of the marts, regarding them as hotbeds of infectious diseases and harbouring unwanted animals.

Breeds

Black calves and black stirks had long been commonplace in the North-East of Scotland, and Shorthorns were by far the most abundant milk cows. Some farms had Ayrshire herds. I was unaware of any Friesian herd in the Aberdeen area during my youth. At that time, some twenty-five breeds of cattle had regional distributions in Britain. Several breeds which were common in their particular regions are now rare, and even the Shorthorn is vulnerable. I saw more Ayrshires on collective farms near Leningrad in 1978, and near Helsinki in 1986, than in Britain. The pied cattle from the Netherlands were introduced to East Anglia early in the twentieth century and are now the most popular dairy breed throughout much of the world. The more recent influx of exotic cattle to Britain favoured muscle rather than milk. Their importation was first sanctioned after a committee, representing breeding societies, deliberated long and often at meetings convened in Paris, of course. Importation started with twenty-five Charolais bulls to artificial insemination centres in 1962. All these Charolais bulls had names with the initial letter "S", their year-of-registration letter. Charolais heifers followed, and Limousin and Simmental arrived in 1972. Perhaps I should explain that, in the course of research, I tested all twenty-five regional breeds standing at the artificial insemination stations from 1957 to 1964, and had my results published in *Heredity*, vol. 20 (1965). I keep my old rope halter as a souvenir, in case it should come in useful!

Cattle feed and treacle

To feed the cattle wintering in the byres, a supply of neeps (Swedish turnips) had to be pulled out of the ground, regardless of mud or ice, and transported in box carts to the muckle shed by the byre. A machine for slicing neeps had a fiercely rotating blade, and was cranked by hand. The cattle were also fed draff, a by-product of the brewing industry. Draff was stored in two large stone troughs, one behind the doocot for the stirks, the other by the end of the dairy byre. The draff was shovelled into a big metal hopper shaped like an old-style pram, and wheeled along the byre at feeding time. At the end of the dairy byre, there was a barrel of black treacle on two trestles. The bung was hammered home to secure the contents. Although the treacle was intended for consumption by cattle, some people were partial to a passing lick. Causey told a story of how he once found a young boy helping himself to a lick of treacle. Causey was worried that the lad would fail to replace the bung firmly and his treacle would run freely, so he encouraged the lad to sup as much as he could, hoping that he would scunner. The following day, the same boy reappeared bringing a very stout pal and said: "Here's a loon will sup yer treacle for ye, Causey".

Grazing

In summer, the dairy herd grazed between milking times. As a boy, I drove the dairy herd to and from the pasture and tethered them in the byre. This early experience in handling cattle stood me in good stead later when I was employed by the Agricultural Research Council.

Milk

The women about the farm hand-milked the dairy cows morning and evening, seven days per week. As milking progressed, Cocker the coobailie carried pairs of pails of milk from the dairy byre down the yard to the dairy. The Health and Safety people demanded that the pails be covered and that Cocker should wear a white coat and cover his unkempt shock of hair – an awkward style for Jock Cocker, who was generally up to his oxters in sharn. He gleefully fed the beasts sculls of neeps, supplied them with forkloads of oat straw, mucked the byre, swept the greep and bedded them down to rest. Yoked between the shafts of a heavily laden, wooden barrow, Cocker would mount a plank to jettison each load of muck on top of the midden. This coobailie afforded us much fun by his comic turn of phrase and frequent malapropisms.

In the dairy, the pails of fresh, warm milk were immediately decanted into a funnel-shaped sieve above the cooler to ripple down over horizontal corrugations on a vertical steel surface and run into ten-gallon, two-handled cans. Cold water flowed within the cooler. A few cans of milk were collected daily from a platform at the roadside and taken by motor lorry to a commercial dairy in Aberdeen. Empty cans were returned daily. A flat wheelbarrow, actually designed for moving peat, was used to transport cans from the farm dairy to the roadside platform. I recall giving my toddler cousin, Eunice, a hurl on this barrow for fun. Eunice enjoyed the sport and demanded more hurls, but the combined weight of our sonsie cousin and the barrow proved too much for my young arms. To my sister Anne and me, the milk platform by the roadside was a theatre stage for our make-believe music-and-dance performances. Anne performed there in a floppy hat and a chiffon net scarf or sash from one of the dresses worn by Mary or Mina at the wedding of John Ronald and our Auntie Jessie in 1934. For my song and dance to our imagined audience, I wore someone's top hat and swagger cane. To this day, Anne and I can't think how we got away with such antics. Perhaps the household were too busy to notice us – or did they?

Butter and cheese

The farmer's wife, my granny, ruled in the farm dairy, which was close to the back door of the farmhouse. Cream was separated out of the milk in the cooler by centrifugal force in a hand-driven separator. To make butter, cream was clamped into a barrel-shaped churn, securely pivoted in a stand and cranked by hand. The contents slapped about within the barrel as it rotated end-on-end. The new butter was divided into weighed portions between two wet wooden bats. Towards the production of cheese, curds were separated in enamel basins and retained in muslin, and pressed within a wooden tub. The cheese press, positioned in the garden outside the dairy wall, had two granite upright supports and a granite crossbar from which a cubic granite weight was suspended by a screw mechanism. Its construction would have done credit to whoever built the Craighead stone circle along the road. Kebbocks at particular stages of maturation were subjected to pressure beneath the stone block, then aligned on a shelf in the dairy to mature. The old press held the secret for making blue crumbly cheese of unsurpassed flavour.

Cheese press, as used widely in North-East Scotland (digital photograph, 2003).

Poultry

Clutches of chickens and ducks were hatched under broody hens, in little hutches and in old barrels. Other clockers were temporarily confined in a wire coop. Larger cohorts of hatchery-reared poultry were introduced to Causeyport as day-old chuckens. The cocks were white with black feathers in their hackles, tails and wings, and the hens were red. This interesting segregation resulted from crossing Rhode Island Red cocks with Light Sussex hens. The sex of the chicks was immediately obvious at hatching. Coloured spiral rings were placed on hens' legs to distinguish the annual broods. Some of the laying hens wandered freely within a big enclosed ree which was wired off in the corner of a nearby field immediately to the south of the steading.

Other poultry roamed the yard in traditional free-range style and were housed near the back of the farmhouse. The birds perched on farm machinery and produced unwanted muck. Dod called farmyard poultry "fowl pests" and said that they all died in debt. The annual flock of turkeys ranged freely. Some of the larger cocks, called "bubblie jocks", made noisy aggressive displays as they reached maturity, and could be quite frightening to young children, such as our cousin Margaret Masson, who was chased into the midden by some. White "bottle-runner" ducks with ridiculous upright carriage contrasted with the familiar and horizontal Khaki Campbells. Broods of ducklings fostered by hens were less likely to find the water in the dam too soon for their healthy development.

Rats, cats and whitrats

Rats and lesser vermin were endemic, particularly in the stacks of oats stored in the corn yard. As threshing progressed, the stacks were reduced and their resident wildlife was exposed. If a stack housed a whitrat (weasel or stoat, locally pronounced "futrat"), the rodents kept at a safe distance. The rats beat tracks between the corn yard and fields and used the drains to move between farms, helping themselves to whatever was available. The menace of vermin was acute where grain was stored and when chickens, ducklings and turkey poults were reared. Cats were important denizens of Causeyport. They converged on the dairy byre at milking time for a sup of fresh, warm milk and scraps of food. Tinned cat food was unknown. One marmalade tom was permitted into the men's kitchen. He sired the attractive tortie female kittens. The population of farm cats was sustained by occasional introductions, acquired by Dod.

The ambition of all the cats was to sneak into the dairy where cream was separated and butter was churned. A legendary "Jean Cat" actually succeeded in gaining entry. Cats were not encouraged in the main living areas of the house, but one enterprising cat kittled in Granny's best hat stored in a box below the bed in the spare bedroom. As a boy, I knew the cats individually and was interested to find new kittens. Some cats cunningly and wisely concealed their offspring from inquisitive youngsters. Some were shy or wild by nature, seldom seen and greatly respected as hunters. I too competed as a ratter. My ratting methods were primitive, far from subtle and certainly illegal by the standards of today, but effective enough to impress my grandfather. Auld Causey had no reputation for generosity, but rewarded me one copper per head each time I laid out a row of my quarry in the close. At that time, the traditional Saturday penny was literally one old penny earned for weekly chores.

Jock and Capens

So far, I have omitted at least two animal species: a daft dog called Jock and a stinking billy goat called Capens. Both these animals afforded amusement. Jock, a big black collie, barked at visitors and noisily pursued passing traffic. On the command "Craws, craws, craws", he would race off barking round the rucks and cause flocks of destructive birds to take flight. Jock was devoid of any useful herding instinct. His predecessor was an Old English sheepdog called Caesar, which featured in old photographs taken using a Kodak Brownie box camera measuring 6 x 5 x 4½ inches. My mother and her next sister Maggie pooled their pocket money to purchase this item from J. Lizars, 171 Union Street, Aberdeen. I now have the same Brownie as a keepsake.

Capens, the goat, had his full share of disgusting habits. His grey coat was greasy to the touch, perpetually saturated in his own urine. He reared up on his hind legs, charged and butted with his horns. Capens owed his presence at Causeyport to a vet who advised that a billy goat about the steading would ward off contagious abortion (*Brucella abortus*) in cattle. I questioned Dod about this curious superstition or incomprehensible form of biological control. Dod said that the unborn calves would have the good sense to stay put, to avoid the stench of the brute.

Livestock health problems

The animals at Causeyport were not free from diseases. A horse contracted grass sickness but survived against the odds, while collapsed cows, suffering from milk fever, were revived by an injection containing calcium. I recall one occasion when a poor cow died, presumably of tuberculosis, and was unceremoniously winched on to the knacker's truck, to the knacker's uncouth commentary. Contagious abortion was known among the cattle; casualties occurred among young turkeys.

11
Wartime

Brief history lesson

For young readers, I outline a bit of historic background as it appeared to me at the age of 11. The League of Nations was formed in 1920 to maintain world peace, but repeatedly failed to stop aggression in the 1930s. Most nations, including Britain, were unprepared for war. The fascists had other ideas, including world conquest. German forces occupied parts of Europe unopposed; but, when the German army invaded Poland, the French and British prime ministers honoured their treaty with Poland and declared war on Germany on 3rd September 1939. The British Expeditionary Force (BEF) went to France. When France was invaded in 1940, most of the BEF retreated and embarked at Dunkirk. Simultaneously, the 51st Highland Division fought a rearguard action to keep France in the war, but were forced to surrender to Rommel's 25th Panzer Regiment at St Valéry-en-Caux, and many remained "in the bag" for the following five years. At that time, both the USA and the Soviet Union remained uncommitted. The prospect of a German invasion of Britain, Hitler's "Operation Sealion", loomed large. Great Britain was militarily and morally isolated in opposition to the aggressors, Germany and Italy (which formed their Axis in June 1940), before Germany invaded Russia in June 1941 and Japan attacked Pearl Harbor in December 1941.

Any account of isolated personal experience distorts the overall situation. This is particularly so in wartime, when information about casualties is suppressed but generally spreads by rumour. Courtesy of Aberdeen Central Library, I have obtained a list of the twenty-eight air raids on Aberdeen (eleven in 1940, fourteen in 1941, two in 1942 and one in 1943). All but three occurred at night, and the majority of the bombs were 500-kg high explosive, while a few were cluster bombs and a few were incendiary bombs. Apart from two memorable exceptions (12th July 1940 and 21st April 1943), most raids were boring interruptions of sleep for those who were not the unfortunate victims. A city is a big target, and it is possible to be fatalistic about the prospect of receiving a direct hit. We had a Morrison shelter at 96 Burns Road. It was like a steel-plate table-top set on girders, designed to prevent a great weight of rubble from falling on those sheltering below it. This was reassuring when droning engines and thumps were heard in the night.

The public were shown how to combat incendiary bombs using a bucket of sand, a stirrup pump and a bucket of water. The pump had two interchangeable spray apertures in its nozzle. The fine spray was played on the burning phosphorus or magnesium to subdue it, then the sand was intended to be placed on the hot bomb to smother it. The crude spray was applied to incidental burning material. The most common incendiary bomb was cylindrical in shape and 30 cm long. Gas masks were carried at all times by everyone.

Physical changes

The physical changes in the countryside were the erection of radar pylons, continuous lines of concrete blocks as tank barriers along all beaches, concrete pill boxes in occasional strategic positions, and the erection of rows of poles wired together across fields and open spaces to deter troops landing in planes or gliders.

The blackout was applied in September 1939, when everyone anticipated air raids. Opaque materials and improvised shutters were used to obscure light from windows. Sticky tape was used to reinforce window panes against bomb blast. All schools were closed until air-raid shelters were built. Protective walls were constructed using sandbags. Children enjoyed filling sandbags with granite dust at Rubislaw Quarry. Robert Gordon's College was the first school to resume classes because a school governor anticipated the need for shelters. He was Colonel Tawse, a prominent building contractor familiar with warfare, so the excellent shelters at Gordon's were designed as covered trenches in the lawn.

One of the many bombs on the last night of raids (on 21st April 1943), a relatively small 50-kg high-explosive bomb, penetrated the quad in front of Robert Gordon's College, between the front door and the school trenches. Sand and stones were sent skywards and did some damage, landing on the surrounding roofs. It is said that the boy firewatchers sleeping in the governors' hall were undisturbed.

Radar

Engineers raised four mysterious prefabricated wooden pylons, section by section, on the high ground west of the Craighead stone circle. In time, the rectangle of wooden pylons was replaced by four taller metal pylons in line parallel with the road towards Badentoy Farm. Similar pylons were erected simultaneously at numerous points along the shores of Britain, at about fifty-mile intervals. These sites were enclosed behind tall fences with sentries posted. We learned later that the pylons supported the antennae of Britain's most timely technical achievement, namely RADAR, which stands for radio detection and ranging.

Wireless

The speeches of Prime Minister Winston Churchill on the wireless inspired a spirit of defiance and hope, although his voice was slurred like that of the boozer he undoubtedly was. Wireless news bulletins were censored by the Ministry of Information. "Lord Haw-Haw", an Irishman speaking on German radio, gave us the German point of view. He seemed more of a joke than a threat. Nevertheless, he was tried by the war-crimes tribunal at Nuremberg after the war and executed as a traitor. At the crucial period in the air battle over south-east England, newsreaders and newspapers presented the score of the respective numbers of Luftwaffe and Royal Air Force planes destroyed during each 24-hour period. We now know that our official score was biased in favour of the RAF due to different fighter pilots unwittingly claiming the same victims. On 7th September 1940, 2,000 civilians were killed in the Blitzkrieg on London and its docklands, but the RAF Spitfires and Hurricanes won the Battle of Britain, the first example of a decisive battle fought in the air.

Raids

Young boys were familiar with the silhouettes of enemy and friendly planes, their top speeds and their armament specifications. They found excitement in the occasional air raids and aerial dogfights. When a particular German plane was shot down over the North Sea, the Causeyport coobailie said that the pilot survived in his rubber *dignity*! On one memorable occasion, 12th July 1940, a Heinkel bomber, from Stavanger in German-occupied Norway, was engaged over Aberdeen by three Spitfires based at Dyce. The population, including young children, left their lunch and callously cheered throughout this engagement, some still with cutlery in their hands! During the continuing air battle, we were unaware that the bomber had hit the Hall Russell shipyard (which no longer exists). The Heinkel droned low in circles above the rooftops. The cross insignia and the gun turrets were very clearly seen. The Spitfires dived in to attack, one after the other. The German gunners retaliated up to their final swoop over the rooftops before being shot down in Anderson Drive between Great Western Road and the old Bridge of Dee. All four crewmen in the bomber perished in a considerable explosion and were buried with military pomp in Allenvale Cemetery.

Blitz

The final raid, at 22:17 on 21st April 1943, is remembered as Aberdeen's blitz. Of the 130 bombs dropped, twelve did not explode. The number of incidents on that night was roughly equivalent to the total for all of the earlier raids. It was bad enough, but not as intense as the Clydebank or Coventry experiences. This final raid coincided with the end of a display of gymnastics by the Boys' Brigade in the Music Hall, Union Street, in which I participated along with the Mannofield BB Company. I was walking homewards with some of the younger boys when the racket started at Holburn Junction, so I decided we should go via the back lane between Union Grove and Albyn Place. We lay face down in the gutter when the debris started to fly about. The high stone walls on both sides of the lane provided protection. We got home safely, apart from Derek Fraser, who opted to go along Holburn Street instead. A boulder came at him like a bouncing rugby ball, and he joined the wounded in hospital.

Local Defence Volunteers

The Foreign Secretary, Mr Anthony Eden, appealed on the wireless for the formation of a Local Defence Volunteer (LDV) force in every community of the kingdom. Hay was made in bright sunshine that day, and Mr Eden's appeal was discussed among the coles. That same evening, a number of local worthies and youths gathered at Banchory-Devenick School. They acquired LDV arm bands but had little in the way of weapons other than a few shotguns. The LDV was soon renamed the Home Guard. A typical army officer, not unlike Captain Mainwaring in the *Dad's Army* TV serial, appeared out of retirement, assumed command and promoted Dod Alexander to platoon sergeant. Dod was the obvious choice, having considerable presence and personality. Arms were desperately scarce. Dod managed to acquire a long-barrelled Browning rifle and some appropriate American ammunition of .300-inch calibre. The open fields around Causeyport presented a wide target area for a sniper with a Browning. Dod saw that his gun had great potential for "sheetin' craws"; but rounds were too scarce.

At first, the Home Guard were a motley lot in working clothes, shouldering improvised weapons until some precious service rifles and cartridges arrived. Later, they were issued with battledress tunics and trousers, leather belts, gaiters and ultimately greatcoats. A military parade was held in Aberdeen. The quartermaster did not have a battledress, belt or Balmoral bonnet large enough to fit Dod, so he paraded along Union Street in working jerkin and tweed cap, carrying the Browning rifle. My mother laughed at the spectacle and teased her young brother, calling him an affront. Weapons training in evening sessions at Banchory-Devenick School taught the platoon how to maintain and use their precious weapons. They learned to name all the parts, strip, clean, lubricate and reassemble them, and clean the barrels using a pullthrough. Ammunition was so precious that aiming and firing was practised by pointing empty weapons at a small target disk with a central aperture. The instructor held the disc in front of one eye while the pupil aimed, squeezed, and pulled the trigger. Although every precaution was taken to ease springs and unload, I wonder if any instructor had his brains blown out by a round left in a breech.

Available shotguns were recommended for night fighting. A tight wire between trees would decapitate unwary enemy motorcyclists. A veteran of the Spanish civil war, a man of unknown allegiance, imparted his repertoire of evil tricks. I sensed that nobody trusted or believed him. Army instructors taught the basic infantry tactics of how to attack using fire and movement. The mnemonic for giving orders was "IIMAC", standing for Information, Intention, Method, Administration, Communication. Needless to say, the intention was invariably to destroy an identified enemy. If the anticipated enemy had landed, the platoon's aim was to attack and inflict the necessary nuisance. At best, the Home Guard would have identified and delayed – a tactical sacrifice, allowing the regular forces to counter-attack. Although the world was impressed by thrusting Panzers and screaming Stuka dive-bombers, technology was primitive in 1940; sweat and toil, blood and tears were expected.

It is now appreciated that German commanders were trying to figure out where to get enough heavy horses to pull their weapons and supplies up British beaches, assuming they ever landed. Fortunately for us, Hitler decided to invade Russia and forgot about invading Britain. It is ironic that the Germans aimed to capture the oilfields in the Caucasus, while the prospect of North Sea gas and oil remained unexplored until thirty years later. The Home Guard was maintained long after the invasion scare subsided. Perhaps its social coherence and camaraderie appealed to the wartime establishment. In retrospect, the air-raid wardens, the emergency fire services and the observers of aircraft proved to be more relevant to the practical situation as it developed.

Chains

At one stage during Hitler's war, the blacksmith at the Banchory-Devenick smiddie worked long hours cutting stout chains into yard lengths then fashioning and attaching big iron rings. He joined one ring to one end of each length of chain. The smith joked that they were our secret weapon. I now understand that many smiths were hard at work up and down the country, and that the pieces of chain were rotated as flails suspended on the fronts of tanks to explode landmines during the North African desert campaign.

Prisoners

As the war progressed, prisoners of war (POWs) were available as labourers on the land. Literally acres of Italian troops had surrendered in Italy's African colonies. Dod was amused by the pranks of some Italian prisoners. One baked a hedgehog wrapped in clay in an open fire. Dod considered most of the Italians too delicate for farm work as he knew it. Following Mussolini's downfall, most Italians were reclassified as co-belligerents – not quite allies. Only the confirmed fascists remained enclosed in prisoner-of-war camps. Most of the German prisoners were captured later in the war. Dod was more favourably impressed by the Germans' capacity for farm work. After the war, the repatriation of prisoners was a slow process, as was the demobilisation of our own forces. Some prisoners remained in the work camps for up to three more years. Some camps were used to accommodate displaced persons, most of whom were eastern Europeans, unwelcome by the post-war regimes in their respective homelands behind the Iron Curtain. These displaced persons were reclassified as European Voluntary Workers (EVW). They lived in camps serviced by the YMCA, and were hired to work on farms. The EVWs were gradually integrated with the British population in the 1950s as the post-war industrial boom developed.

12

My grandparents (generation "5")

Auld Causey

It is customary for farmers to be nicknamed according the name of their farm. My mother's father, George Alexander (senior), was disrespectfully known as "Auld Causey". This nickname provides clear identification wherever the name recurs throughout the genealogy. Auld Causey was already nearly 74 when I first saw the light of day in 1927. He farmed Causeyport to a ripe old age, retired at the age of 90, and died in 1946, aged 92, when I was 18.

The first of three tables attached at the end of this account traces Auld Causey's ancestry. George Alexander was born in 1853 at Mill of Findon, Portlethen. In 1895, as a bachelor aged 41, he married Ann Paterson Ritchie (1872–1961), aged 22, a spinster and farmer's daughter from Mains of Findon. Banns were according to the forms of the Church of Scotland, and Mary Jane Ritchie, a sister of the bride, was a witness. The groom was just five years junior to the bride's father, his close neighbour. Two different sepia-tone prints show the wedded couple – one in their wedding attire, the other contrived in an Aberdeen studio some time after the wedding. It was early days for photography. The couple were required to pose motionless for the duration of a time exposure in front of a plate camera. Auld Causey would sooner have used the time to sow crops. Both photos are presented here, and the reader is invited to interpret them.

Wedding of George Alexander and
Ann Paterson Ritchie (1895).

Studio portrait of George Alexander
and Ann Paterson Ritchie (1895).

Causey the entertainer

Auld Causey was a big fish in a small sea – an extrovert with a good, powerful voice, given to loud spontaneous outbursts of song, such as:

> Oh Hielan' Rory, did she come frae Tobermory?
> Can she say "hooch aye" an' "cummerrachum-choo"?
> Will she row me in the heather like when we were boys together
> Singing "Oh! cummer-ree, cummer-roo"?

or

> I'm ninety-four this mornin', aye I'm ninety-four today.
> I'm nae so young as I used to be, I'm gettin' old and grey.
> But my heart is young and I'm fond o' fun, and I'm very proud to say
> That I'm gettin' married on Thursday tho' I'm ninety-four today.

He clearly belonged to the age of family entertainment, village-hall concerts and music halls. He loved to sing the then popular ballads and comic songs – "Tobermory", "Ohio", "O'er the Hills to Ardentinny", "She is my Daisy", "The Last of the Sandies" and "Fou the Noo", composed and sung by Sir Harry Lauder; "I'm Ninety-four this Mornin'" and "I Belang tae Glasgow" by Will Fyffe; "I'll Gang tae Paisley" by Arthur Lloyd; and "Hielan' Rory" by W. F. Frame. Causey was sometimes accompanied on piano by his daughter Ann, my late mother, who was Auntie Annie to many of my generation. Along with my mother's collection of music, I inherited Causey's copies of sheet-music scores together with the original verbal patter associated with certain pieces. One of my sister Isobel's few childhood memories of the old man is of him belting out "Annie Laurie" to our mother's piano accompaniment.

Causey took part in the local amateur dramatic society, and his favourite musical was "Mains' Wooing", in which he performed about 1920 playing the lead role of Mains. Our mother also had a part in the production held in the village hall, which must have been quite an occasion in the community. All this stopped temporarily during the Great War (1914–18).

During the early part of the war, in November 1915, Jean Ritchie, one of Granny's sisters, was married. Our mother recalled the great preparations for the reception held in the barn at the Mains of Findon. The place was scrubbed and decked out for the occasion, and no doubt Auld Causey entertained with a few songs. Sadly, the bridegroom died only four weeks after the wedding, two weeks after his six-month illness had taken a turn for the worse. Our Auntie Mary, then aged 11, was sent to live with the 26-year-old widow for a while. In October 1919, Jean followed her sister Peg in emigrating to the USA (Maryland/Washington DC area), where they both married Park brothers who also hailed from Portlethen. Their descendants appeared to have lost touch with the families on this side of the Atlantic; but Ivor has been taking steps to trace and visit them.

Grace

On occasions when three generations dined together in the Causeyport farmhouse on twelve-place, heirloom, "Foley" china, Causey would say grace before the meal. In respectful mood, he would recite the following:

> "The Selkirk Grace"
>
> Some ha'e meat, and canna eat,
> And some wad eat that want it;
> But we ha'e meat, and we can eat,
> And sae the Lord be thankit. Amen.
>
> (Burns)

If Causey felt less than serious, he would recite this doggerel, attributed to Causey:

> Grace be here, Grace be there,
> And Grace be o'er this table.
> Let ilka ane tak up a speen,
> And sup for a' 'e's able. Amen.

I fondly recall the "free-range" hen broth and clootie mealie dumpling and skirlie served on such occasions. I still salivate at the thought of all those home-bred, home-grown and home-cooked products, which tasted so superior to their modern "rubber-duck" equivalents.

Education

Causey's preference for sons was purely selfish. Family members at home worked for a pittance. This attitude may have been shared by most farmers at that time. Causey did not encourage higher education, but by contrast his neighbour and father-in-law, William A. Ritchie at the Mains of Findon, had a more generous outlook. He was active on the school board, held spelling bees for farm workers and encouraged those with ability to pursue education. For example, two of his sons, William and John, were high-flying civil servants, as described earlier. In retrospect, Causey took some pride in his daughter Jessie becoming a teacher, and boasted that all of his family were equally able at school.

I had no reason to think that Causey was particularly devout; I suspect he was more at ease in a mill, mart, smiddie or village hall than at the Kirk. Nevertheless, the family had a box pew in Portlethen Kirk. I suspect that family worship was motivated by Granny.

Wet Review

Causey was the "life and soul" in his time, particularly with Queen Victoria's "Volunteers", the prototype of the Territorial Army. He enjoyed competitive shooting at wapenshaws, and he was present at the "Wet Review" (1881), when all the volunteers were mustered for inspection by Her Majesty Queen Victoria in the Queen's Park by Holyrood Palace, Edinburgh, in a torrential rainstorm. In 1931, Causey attended a "Wet Review" veterans' reunion. He was introduced, as the oldest survivor of the review, to the then Duchess of York (the now deceased Queen Mother). The Duchess complimented him on his state of preservation. Causey replied: "You are a gey bonny lass yourself, and if I were a bit younger I would fancy courtin' you". Deference was not any part of Causey's makeup. A reporter from the *Bulletin* newspaper overheard the conversation and asked Causey how he dared to be so familiar. Hence the headline "North-east man 'wasna feart'" appeared above Causey's portrait in the *Bulletin*. I still have a glossy copy of this press photograph of the bemedalled Causey in a suit, a gold watch chain looping his waistcoat, Anthony Eden hat, white moustache and white hankie in his breast pocket (see frontispiece). Causey's reminiscences of Queen Victoria's volunteers got some wry responses from the veterans of the next generation, Kitchener's volunteers, who saw active service against the Kaiser's men and the Turks. For example, Causey's son-in-law Sam Jamieson and other diehards joked about the fictitious battle of Clochandighter, that being the site of the local shooting range.

Causey the autocrat

Auld Causey had a reputation as an autocrat, and apparently he used to stand at his bedroom window at the back of the house, overlooking the farmyard, and shout his orders to the men below. This shows his contempt for the hired men and their cringing acceptance of his authority, as he should have given his orders face to face in the stableyard.

Single malt

I recall an occasion when my father, Sam Jamieson, asked me to smuggle a cutter of malt whisky to his elderly father-in-law, who was ill in bed. This was delivered as advised, without a word to Granny. The old man tucked the gift under his pillow. Unfortunately, a dribble of the contents leaked into his feather bed. Granny was not amused. Other members of the household thought it highly comical. I made my presence scarce to avoid the wrath and ridicule.

Clock

On another occasion, the old man was lying awake in bed in the wee sma' 'oors and judging the time by the chimes of the grandfather clock on the stair landing. The clock stopped. It was dark, and Causeyport had no electricity. Causey went to wind up the weight of the clock and must have misjudged his balance. Both grandfather and grandfather clock slid down a flight of stairs to the hall. The clock case was in small pieces in a heap of sawdust and woodworm, but the old man in his nightshirt insisted that he was none the worse.

The roup

Latterly, Causey used two walking sticks for support. He became increasingly dependent on his younger son, Dod, who managed the farm work at Causeyport up to the roup in 1943, when Causey retired to "Lochnagar", Muchalls. I attended the roup. On that day, Causey, aged 90, went out into the crowded farm close without a jacket. Granny severely chastised him for his stupidity. (It was not unusual for Causey to rejoice in a shower of rain in the growing season, his shirt soaking wet, viewing his fields of swelling neeps and spuds.) Causey's elder son John replaced the jacket on Causey's shoulders, but it was discarded on the ground. Such was the despairing reaction of Causey witnessing the dispersal of all his beasts and possessions.

The auctioneer at the roup sold off all the livestock, implements, some furniture and odds and ends with great style and humour. As was the custom, drams of whisky were dispensed among good purchasers. Among the many things which vanished without trace that day was a family Bible in which factual information about antecedents was recorded in copperplate handwriting. This Bible was kept in the drawing-room. It is sad to think that this record of family history may have gone as waste paper. Fortunately, much of this information has been extracted in recent years from official sources, particularly by cousins John Alexander, Sandy Caple, Mrs Laura Sutherland, Mrs Pat Martin and Ivor Normand, to name a few.

The pewter which had been used by the farm servants at Causeyport since the Alexander family moved there in 1904, and probably used earlier, was regarded as old rubbish in 1943, when Auntie Mary disposed of loads of accumulated junk before the roup. Mary buried all the pewter in the peat moss, which had clumps of heather and wet bogs where peat had been worked. The moss may have developed into natural woodland by now. Cousin Eunice, who admires old pewter, wonders how valuable the same pewter would be today.

Funeral

I attended Causey's funeral in March 1946, when I was an 18-year-old lance-corporal on leave from Whittington Barracks near Lichfield, Staffordshire. The six pallbearers at his burial in Portlethen kirkyard were his two sons John and Dod; two of his four sons-in-law, George Gray (a police sergeant, married to Maggie) and "Aixie" Masson (a Catterline salmon fisher, married to Mina); and his two eldest grandsons, John Alexander (elder son of John senior) and myself. At that time, there was no road up to the top level of the kirkyard; the coffin was carried manually up a steeply inclined footpath. Causey's physique was as becomes a miller used to lifting great sacks of grain and scoops of meal. Like the rest of the family, there was a lot of him. The rear pair of bearers, my cousin John and I, were the shortest in stature. We had to push hard into our boots as the load tilted back on the steep brae, but it was our privilege to carry Causey. The burial ended an era in the history of the family. Large men shed a few silent tears at the graveside, but the mood soon lightened; the nonagenarian was released from the physical humiliations of age.

The gravestone inscription reads: "Erected in loving remembrance of my husband George Alexander, farmer, late of Causeyport, Portlethen, who died at Muchalls, 23rd March 1946, aged 92 years. Also in loving memory of our mother Ann Paterson Ritchie, wife of the above, who died at Dryden Cottage, Stonehaven, 20th Sept. 1961, aged 89 years".

Two long generation gaps separate Causey from me. Nevertheless, George Alexander, miller and farmer, made a lasting impression. Come to think of it, as each of his twenty grandchildren got a random, one in four, selection of Causey's genes, perhaps we should take a closer look at ourselves, particularly if we are spared to compete with his longevity.

Inventory

The inventory of the estate of George Alexander, retired farmer, "Lochnagar", Muchalls, was lodged with the sheriff clerk at Stonehaven. The net heritable and movable estate as reported in the *Press and Journal* was £22,793. It is well that he was not a poor man, because Granny came into the "ten-bob widow" category. They were born too soon to contribute to, or reap the benefits of, the welfare state as enjoyed by the following generation.

My Granny

Table 2 at the end of this narrative traces my maternal grandmother's forebears. Ann Paterson Ritchie (1872–1961) was the eldest of eight children of the farmer in the Mains of Findon. The land at Mains of Findon lay adjacent to that at the Mill of Findon, farmed by my grandfather, who boasted that he did not go far to find his wife – "just o'er the dyke". George was 42, Ann 23 years of age, when their eldest child, Annie (Ann Paterson Alexander, my mother), was born at the Mill of Findon in November 1895. Maggie (1897), John (1899), Jessie (1902) and Mary (1904) were also born at the Mill of Findon. Dod (1906) and Mina (1910) were born after the family moved to Causeyport Farm (see also Table 3).

My mother's mother looked the real traditional granny, keeping her hair in a bun by day and a plait in the evening. She wore a knitted shawl in natural wool. Looking back, I have to agree with my sister Anne that Granny made no physical demonstration of affection towards us. I never expected it. Perhaps the native dourness hardens early at Causeyport. But Granny and I had good rapport. Her severe appearance was deceptive. She composed verse for family occasions, had an astute sense of humour and was always aware of current events. A back problem caused Granny to stoop. I suspect this was the result of some neglected injury; but she did not complain.

I remember Granny with pails and stool, milking a number of cows by hand, morning and evening, as did the other women about the farm – but Granny always tackled the most nervous and awkward cows. The farm dairy was the centre of her working life. Her butter and her dry, crumbly, blue-vein cheese were highly acclaimed by mature and experienced tasters, as were her girdle scones, pancakes and oatcakes, all baked over the open hearth. Each girdle-sized oatcake was cut into four segments. These quarters curved slightly while they were set up on their edge to finish the baking process in a frame surrounding the fire. Large quantities of oatcakes were stored in the meal girnel in the men's kitchen and eaten ad lib. Granny still baked scones, pancakes and crumpets when she was in her eighties.

Granny had her own stall in the Green in Aberdeen on Friday market days to sell her own labelled "Causeyport Butter". A shelt yoked to a gig transported her produce until this transport was replaced by an early Morris car. She personally sold her dairy produce on the Green up to about 1930, when she contracted to sell her labelled produce through an Aberdeen grocer who had a permanent shop at the Green. My mother, Mrs Ann Jamieson, sometimes pushed two young bairns (Anne and me) in a pram from her tenement house at 37 Mount Street down to the Green to purchase her mother's produce. This habit was discontinued. The Causeyport butter was no cheaper than elsewhere!

As my sister Isobel recalls, Granny was a gifted needlewoman who made her husband's shirts with beautifully hand-done buttonholes and with collars that always sat well when worn. Their daughters were brought up to be good needlewomen, often working fine stitchery by the light of a paraffin lamp. Once, when our mother was in her late teens, she was *ordered* late at night to attend the laying-out of a relative who had died. To us, this seems a barbaric experience for someone who had not seen a corpse before, but this was the custom. There had been no question of rebelling against this "request", as our Granny was a pretty autocratic lady and had to be up early for the milking. Another tale of Granny's severity was when our mother was severely rebuked for singing while milking on a Sunday evening. It was one thing working on the Sabbath, but another thing singing while you worked.

Mary Jane Alexander, Causey's spinster daughter, cared for both her parents after they retired to "Lochnagar", Muchalls, where Causey died in 1946. Mary and her mother moved to Dryden Cottage, 3 Robert Street, Stonehaven, a charming old house a short distance west of the square. This ancient house had a large and neglected walled garden which Mary restored to fruition. At Dryden Cottage, Granny did not have a good word for the electric cooker. She cooked skink (soup) on the open fire in the back living-room. The term "skink" is now applied to a stew soup using a hough or knuckle of beef. No lizard is involved.

I always visited my grandmother at Dryden on my occasional trips north from Birmingham, Cambridge and Edinburgh. On one occasion, I found her reading a large-print version of the Bible (King James' version), revelling in some wicked stories in the Old Testament. My venerable Granny spent her remaining years in Dryden Cottage and died there of bronchial pneumonia in 1961 at the age of 89. I attended her funeral and was privileged to hold a cord at her burial in Portlethen kirkyard.

Auntie Mary inherited Dryden Cottage, which she sold in 1983 to purchase a smaller house, Ocean View Cottage, 33a Robert Street. The purchaser of Dryden renovated the cottage and split the plot up for additional residential development. The Dryden property was advertised as "nestling in a large and delightful secluded garden only minutes from the centre of Stonehaven. The garden is very pleasantly laid out and productive yet with ample space for extension of the cottage or another house. Cottage comprises, on the ground floor, porch, hall, spacious lounge, double bedroom, living room and kitchen, and on the first floor, two double bedrooms, box room and bathroom. Range of outhouses. Prices over £45,000."

13

Seven siblings in generation "6"

1/7 Ann (Annie)

A stone at Portlethen kirkyard reads: "In loving memory of our parents, Samuel Jamieson, died 18th Feb. 1959 aged 62 years, and Ann Paterson Alexander, died 29th March 1986 aged 90 years". My mother was the eldest child of George (Auld Causey) Alexander and Ann Paterson Ritchie. My father, Samuel Jamieson, was the elder son of James (Jimmie) Jamieson, who worked on the Craigievar estate and at Balquharn Farm, Portlethen, and Martha Jamieson (born Dunn) from Leochel-Cushnie. Martha died at Howeburn Cottage, close to MacBeth's Cairn, Lumphanan, in 1936. Jimmie Jamieson died at Tillylair Farm, Lumphanan, in 1951.

Up to the age of 14, my parents attended the same class in Portlethen School, taught finally by Dominie Hunter, who ruled with a rod of iron (or at least the tawse). During our mother's schooldays, there was a much overgrown pet lamb which followed her (and Maggie and John) to school. Dominie Hunter sent her home with it. Sam and Ann's school certificates, dated 1910, read as follows:

> The Lords of the Committee of the Privy Council on Education in Scotland have been pleased to sanction the award of this Certificate of Merit, in terms of Article 29 of the Scotch Code, by the Managers of Portlethen Public School, Banchory-Devenick, to [*named pupil*] of fourteen years of age in that School.

A studio portrait of the author's mother, Ann P. Alexander (c. 1920), was kept in his father's pocketbook.

The reverse side of the document listed English, Arithmetic, Handwriting, Laws of Health, Money Matters, Nature Study, Geometry and Mensuration, Scale Drawing. Sewing for girls replaced Drill, Land Surveying and Navigation for boys. My parents' school records were remarkably parallel and very commendable, but Ann had "excellent" for money matters whereas Sam had "very good". This difference became a household joke in that my father always disputed Dominie Hunter's assessment of my mother's money sense. Ann's ability at Portlethen school was recognised by Dominie Hunter, who encouraged her to continue in education; but her mother needed her in 1910 to help bring up the six younger siblings and to work at Causeyport. Ann acted as unpaid nursemaid, since her own mother was much too busy with her other duties – milking twice a day, looking after the poultry, and making butter and cheese to sell at a stall on the Green in Aberdeen on Fridays, to name but a few.

My mother worked at Causeyport from leaving school, aged 14 in 1910, until she married my father in July 1925. She later confided to my sister, Isobel, that she was sadly disappointed when required to work at home instead of going up to the Mackie Academy in Stonehaven. Instead, she had to rock the wooden cradle containing the infant Mina, born in March 1910. The rocking motion was normally achieved by pulling on a string, and sometimes by giving it a resentful kick. Our mother also admitted that she was envious of Jessie attending the Mackie from about 1917. Nevertheless, Ann and Jessie remained close friends and wrote to each other throughout their adult lives, with Jessie visiting often from her home in Yorkshire. Our mother commented that Jessie's last few letters were atypically confused – the first sad indication of Jessie's decline.

As my father's father was a farm labourer, higher education was not a real option for Sam, who was to follow a different career, described below. The ex-classmates, Sam and Ann, married in 1925 when both were aged 29, after Ann had had fifteen years of toil at home, including four years of war. By then, Sam was a partner in a haulage and warehousing business. They had four children: my sisters Anne (1926), Isobel (1931) and Edith (1934), and me in 1927. Respectively, they became a secretary/typist, teacher, pharmacist, and research fellow in genetics.

In 1931, the Jamieson family moved within Aberdeen from 37 Mount Street to 96 Burns Road, a semi-detached bungalow built of Rubislaw granite on the west side of town. This newly built house cost £450 cash in 1931. The original accommodation was three rooms plus kitchen, coalhouse and bathroom. The structure was substantial. The services were considered sufficient at the time, but expectations were modest compared with now. A back boiler behind the coal fire heated the water. My mother tended an open fire all her life and failed to understand how people could possibly live without one. The flush toilet was indoors in the bathroom. The bath, basin and tubs had hot and cold taps. The twin tubs supported a wringer. A mangle was obtained, then a hand-driven "Jiffy" washing machine. An immersion heater and electric fire were luxuries added at a later date. The three 15-amp power points, one to each room, and the new electric lights were a novelty and used sparingly. A piano was the first luxury, followed by the treadle sewing machine, which we treasure to this day and which became a household essential.

Two bedrooms were added later in the loft as the family grew. In due course, an outdoor coalhouse, garage, greenhouse and back porch were added. The garden soil at Burns Road contained many stones, most of which were gradually removed during sustained cultivation. A ton of Shore Porters' horse manure dug in each winter resulted in a rich crop of spuds and vegetables towards making broth. After we children had made our own way in life, my mother was free to develop a happy social life with the Church and the Townswomen's Guild. My mother was one of a group of ladies who went to London to celebrate the Coronation in 1953. In particular, she convened a ladies' choir. They enjoyed entertaining old people living in residential homes. Latterly, some of the entertainers were a deal older than some of the auld bodies in their audiences!

Anne, who remained resident in Aberdeen after the rest of us dispersed, visited our ageing mother daily. Twenty-seven years after our father's death, our mother died of cancer of the intestine, at the age of 90, in March 1986. Her last weeks were spent in Roxburghe House, a Deeside hospice. She was mentally alert, courageous, even entertaining, up to her death. After her funeral, many friends and relatives gathered together in the Mannofield Hotel. The ashes of our parents are in the annexe graveyard of Portlethen Kirk. I am now the registered holder of that plot numbered 90.

Samuel Jamieson (Dad)

Lord Kitchener's finger-pointing poster, "Your country needs you", called for 100,000 volunteers to enlist in the regular army in August 1914. Sam, aged 17, volunteered with the rest. He served from 1914 to 1919 in Egypt, Palestine and the Balkans. (I am now the keeper of his 1914 star and other medals.) Conscription was introduced later, and Sam's call-up papers were posted. The military police, called "redcaps", suspected that he was hiding in the Craigievar woods. My grandmother, Martha Jamieson, showed them a photograph of her son in uniform in Egypt. Although Sam survived the entire war unharmed, he had the misfortune to contract malaria and dysentery after the armistice was signed in 1919. At the time, quinine was the only treatment for malaria. Sam was reduced to skin and bone. On discharge, he returned to farm labour for two years to restore his health and strength.

Shore Porter

In 1921, Sam was elected a member of the Shore Porters' Society, Aberdeen, having purchased a £300 share of the horse and plant. The Shories are haulage contractors and bonded warehouse-keepers. In modern parlance, the members call themselves directors. The Society was officially founded in 1498, although this ancient craft existed earlier. In the past, uniformed porters, wearing frock coats and tamoshanters, ran sedan chairs for gentle ladies. Up to about 1950, Shories were hired as pallbearers by prominent local families. The continuing existence of this firm is attributed in some measure to its rule which excludes nepotism. Sons of members are not eligible to become members. Fortunately for me, other career opportunities were available, mainly because my parents allowed me to enjoy secondary education. I later qualified for an ex-service grant towards higher education. During my father's thirty-eight years as a Shorie, the Society survived three crises – the General Strike (1926), the Second World War and the post-war nationalisation of road transport.

General Strike

During the General Strike, the drivers were allowed to transport food, and owners were permitted to transport their own goods. The strike pickets challenged the haulage of casks of whisky from the bonded warehouses to Aberdeen's pubs. On such occasions, the partners claimed that liquor was food and delivered it personally, helped by a big, swack, high-stepping shelt.

War years

In 1939, the Shories' splendid fleet of Albion motor wagons was commandeered to go to France with the British Expeditionary Force (BEF). Sadly, the lorries were abandoned to the enemy, on the beach at Dunkirk, when the BEF were evacuated. My cousin, Harry, saw these lorries on the beach but had no opportunity to scorch them. The firm's insignia had not been concealed by camouflage paint. For public morale, the Dunkirk debacle was presented as a tactical retreat. Meanwhile, the Shories' horse-drawn capability was restored to twenty-two Clydesdales, a grey Percheron, a Belgian horse and a big shelt.

The whisky bonds and the stables were particularly vulnerable during air raids. To reduce the risk from incendiary bombs, the top floor of each bond was emptied and given a layer of sand. Some roofs were broken by bomb debris, but no fire resulted. The Shories' horses were stabled in Cotton Street, dangerously close to the gasworks. A roster of firewatchers slept there in a loose box converted to a bothy. They passed the time playing dominoes. Fortunately for the city population, and the animals, there was neither whisky firestorm nor gas inferno in Aberdeen. We can forget about the near misses.

Sam was an acknowledged judge of the "soundness of wind and limb" in horses. On behalf of his business partners, he purchased five-year-old geldings on farms. The Shories' horses were always well groomed and made a powerful impression, clattering along the cobbled streets and quays, in black polished leather harness, high pointed collars, shining steel-piked haims and steel chains. Their workaday turnout was like present-day show-ring competition. They were a fine advertisement in an area where many of the population were linked to the farming community. Sam was enthusiastic about horses and cared for their health and comfort. He inspected the stables in the evenings and at weekends. He maintained that horse transport, without road tax, was commercially competitive for short distances about the town; but the real limiting factor was the availability of conscientious and experienced horsemen.

Incidentally, the horse manure, which was stored in a pit in the stable building in Cotton Street, was purchased in bulk by a firm of mushroom-growers and transported to Sussex by train.

Boxmaster

Sam Jamieson was repeatedly elected "Boxmaster", the office of the Shorie gaffer who ordered the carters, motormen and labourers about their daily tasks. Occasionally, he employed me as a casual labourer; my best rate of pay was one shilling and ninepence per hour in 1951, carrying bags of flour and stowing them ten high in a stuffy warehouse. I learned at first hand that most workmen respected Sam as one who expected a fair day's work for a fair day's pay, but some wags told me that my father was a bloody slavedriver. Well, I could have told them that. Be that as it may, he laughed that one off and slaved along with the rest. To give him his credit, he did not ask any man to do any task that he could not, and did not, do himself. The age of sweat and toil was not quite over during his time. The Shories had a proud tradition of physical prowess. They led the work by example, but in retrospect they should have been kinder to themselves.

British Road Services

Clement Attlee's Labour Party ousted Winston Churchill's government in the 1945 election, just before the end of the war. The nationalisation of road transport was one of Labour's revolutionary changes. The state officials who bought out the private transport businesses balked at the cost of buying the bonded warehouses, which were an integral part of Shorie business. Fortunately, the Shories had purchased the freehold of the bonded warehouses when the Aberdeen Town Council went bankrupt in 1805 following their ambitious construction of the viaduct which now forms Union Street. The Shories remained a private company and found that they were well able to compete with the bureaucratic British Road Services.

Lifestyle

My father enjoyed his garden. He belonged to the men's club at Mannofield Church. He played golf using an antique set of hickory-shafted clubs and was a founder member of the Seafield bowling club. His family car was never used for business. My father fancied the farms and forests of Deeside and Donside. Dad's unfulfilled wish was to return to the soil, taking my mother and me along with him of course. Neither my mother nor I favoured his idea, for our independent reasons. Mum did not relish the prospect of returning to brookie pots and kettles on an open range. I already had a mind to study biology. Instead of taking a farm, Dad generously helped his sister Bella and her family to rent, stock, farm and later buy Tillylair Farm, Lumphanan. My grandfather, Jimmie Jamieson, was well cared for there in his latter years. My late cousin, Robert Emslie, to his credit, became laird of Tillylair. The same prospect was available to me after demobilisation, but I followed my own curious interests.

It was my father's habit to cycle home, from the quay to Burns Road, for his midday meal. After eating, he would gulp half a cup of tea and dash off because men were standing, waiting to be told what to do. My mother often told him to slow down because, as she said, the men would be waiting there after he was dead. Sure enough, in 1959, Samuel Jamieson collapsed at work, due to cerebral thrombosis. He lay severely paralysed in Foresterhill Hospital for several weeks before dying there at the age of 62.

2/7   Margaret ("Auntie Maggie")

Causey's second-born, Margaret Hay Alexander, was born in 1897 and died in 1972 aged 74. Maggie attended Burnett's business school in Aberdeen, and found a secretarial appointment in Aberdeen. In 1924, Maggie married Police Constable George Gray, who was born at Leochel-Cushnie in 1899. He was Police Sergeant at Police Headquarters, Lodge Walk, by the Castlegate, before he retired from the service in 1951. He then worked for seventeen years as a meat inspector at Lawson of Dyce. He died in Aberdeen in 1980, aged 80. George and Maggie are buried in Springbank Cemetery, Aberdeen, beside their beloved son Dennis, who died of streptococcal tonsillitis aged 3 years in 1933.

3/7   Uncle John ("Johnnie")

A stone in Portlethen kirkyard commemorates Lizzie Rennie, Mains of Scotstown, died 2 Oct. 1967 aged 67, and John Bruce Alexander, North Brae, died Crathes 26 June 1986 aged 86.

John, elder son of Auld Causey, was born at the Mill of Findon and moved to Causeyport as a child aged 5 years. When he reached school-leaving age, John was required to work for his father at Causeyport. His maternal grandfather, William Ritchie at Mains of Findon, recognised John's potential. As he put it, "The lad has a good head on his shoulders". Causey uncompromisingly ridiculed his father-in-law's suggestion about education, saying: "He will be a farmer". This he did – and a highly successful farmer to boot. John left Causeyport as a young man to work elsewhere. He also served in the Gordon Highlanders as a "Black and Tan" in Ireland. He later farmed dairy cows at Badentoy Farm, then beef cattle at Mains of Scotstown near Bridge of Don, Aberdeen. The Scotstown Farm buildings have been partly reconstructed, but the surrounding land is now built up to take the overflow of population from Aberdeen.

Siblings of John's told me that Causey required his son to sow neep seed in the Langstane park at Causeyport while on army leave. They recalled John with a horse-drawn turnip-sowing machine at midnight, and Causey walking alongside carrying a lantern. Nobody explained to me whether this desperation was prompted by shortage of labour due to war casualties, or maybe an awkward spell of weather. Still, this scene may epitomise the relationship between father and son.

Speculation

We may speculate on why John left Causeyport at an early stage in his career to work elsewhere as a hired man. In due course, John returned to Causeyport to persuade his father to help him into

Badentoy Farm (170 acres, supporting 111 dairy cattle). According to my late mother, the father and son retired to the front room at Causeyport and engaged in a long and heated conversation behind the closed door. John emerged with the help he required. In my recall, Badentoy Farm was absolutely heaving with milk cattle. On my few visits to Badentoy, it appeared to me that Uncle John spent all his time hand-milking cattle. A large man hand-milking was an unusual sight in my experience. John could milk a cow in five minutes.

High Court

A shepherd at an Aberdeen mart accused John of improperly including, among his lot for sale, some sheep that were alleged to belong to a neighbour. John was indignant at this accusation, and called in the police. This backfired: John was tried in the High Court in Aberdeen, charged with sheep-stealing. The verdict was "not proven", but in effect this inconclusive verdict was most unsatisfactory. John and his family remain transparently honest in all their dealings.

A short time after the court case, I visited his elderly mother, my Granny, at Dryden Cottage, Stonehaven. I wondered if family members had tried to withhold the news, and did not raise the subject. However, I soon learned that Granny, being an avid reader of the *Press and Journal*, was well informed and in good humour about the court case. The first thing she said to me was: "I see Johnnie has been in a bit of trouble. Were folk hanged for sheep-stealing?"

John Alexander and Lizzie Rennie had five children, namely Margaret, John, Isobel, Eleanor and George, and now there are numerous grandchildren and great-grandchildren.

4/7   Auntie Jessie

Stones at Portlethen and at Banchory-Devenick record the loving memory of Jessie Brechin Alexander, who died 11th May 1989 aged 87 years, beloved wife of John Ronald, who died 30th March 1992 aged 90 years. They were each other's fourth cousins in the Paterson line.

By the time Auntie Jessie was old enough to leave Portlethen School, Granny had sufficient help at home from her eldest daughter, Ann, who was then about 22 years of age. It was Granny's idea that Jessie should continue her education at the Mackie Academy in Stonehaven. Jessie said that she cried all the way on the train on her first day. It was the first time she had been so far alone. It is difficult to believe that the same timid teenager became the confident young teacher at Banchory-Devenick School, journeying there by motorcycle from Causeyport. For most of her career, Jessie taught children at Huttons Ambo, a village near Malton, between York and Scarborough. They lived in the school house and were well integrated in the life of the village. Jessie was active in the Women's Rural Institute (WRI), always involved in different handicrafts, and organising others about her to do likewise. Malingerers such as I, who did not feel the need for this physiotherapy, had to take evasive action.

John Ronald was the son of the farmer at Batchart Farm, Blairs. He was employed later by the English Milk Marketing Board. John and Jessie retired to Norton-on-Derwent, near Malton, Yorkshire. They are survived by their daughter Eunice, now twice widowed. She has four grown-up children and, at the latest count, eight grandchildren.

5/7   Auntie Mary

Mary and her youngest sister, Mina, share a grave at Portlethen. The stone is inscribed: "In loving memory of Mary Jane Alexander, late of Stonehaven, born at Mill of Findon, Portlethen, 4th May 1904, died 4th February 1995, a dear sister and aunt. Williamina Ritchie Alexander born Causeyport 1910 died 1998, relict of James Masson, Catterline, a loving wife and mother."

Four sisters celebrating the golden wedding of Jessie and John Ronald in 1984. Left to right: Miss Mary Jane Alexander, Mrs J. Masson (Williamina Ritchie Alexander), Mrs S. Jamieson (Ann Paterson Alexander), Mrs J. Ronald (Jessie Brechin Alexander). (Photographer: Robert D. Smith.)

Two brothers celebrating the golden wedding of Jessie and John Ronald in 1984. Left to right: George ("Dod") Alexander, John Bruce Alexander. (Photographer: Robert D. Smith.)

Mary remained by her parents for as long as they lived. At Causeyport, she hand-milked kye, kept poultry and worked in the kitchen. Mary moved with her parents to "Lochnagar", Muchalls, where she helped to nurse her father, then to Dryden Cottage, Stonehaven, where she helped her mother. Mary enjoyed the challenge of restoring the neglected garden at Dryden Cottage, which she duly inherited. She moved into a smaller house at "Ocean View", Robert Street, Stonehaven, where she lived to the age of 90. The family was well represented at her funeral and afterwards at the Hillside Hotel, Portlethen, where numerous cousins were reunited after many years. Mary was a thrifty woman. Fetteresso Kirk and her twenty nieces and nephews were the beneficiaries of her estate. God bless Auntie Mary.

Auntie Mary was most curious to know what I was up to as a postgraduate in Birmingham. She decided that, as nobody could explain my activities, I couldn't be up to any good. In fact, I had a Colonial Office studentship to research the genetics of the swarming habits of African locusts. On hearing that I was working on locust control, Great-Aunt Peg (Margaret Park, née Ritchie) in Washington DC said she had the answer: "It is easy to keep down crickets. Keep plenty of chickens."

6/7   George (Uncle Dod)

A stone at Portlethen Kirk reads: "In loving memory of George Alexander, late of Stonehaven, born Causeyport 19th July 1906, died 23rd March 1991, beloved husband and father. Also his wife, Helen Findlay, born Upper Brandsmyres, Banchory-Devenick, 11th February 1913, died 16th January 1999, dear mother and grandmother". George was widely known as Dod, sometimes called "Dod Causey". Dod, as an abbreviation of George, is commonly used in Scotland, but unknown in South Britain. Dod's wife, Helen, was always called Dolly. I know not why; I never asked, just accepted.

On frequent visits to Causeyport Farm between 1931 and 1943, I often latched on to Causey's younger son, my Uncle Dod, who patiently answered my questions about farm crops, livestock and implements. This tall, muscular man was grieve of Causeyport up to the roup (displenish sale by auction) in 1943. Thereafter, Dod farmed Glithno, then Mains of Ury, both near Stonehaven, and later he lived at Clashfarquhar near Portlethen. Brothers Dod and John purchased Glithno Farm as a joint enterprise. They drove seventy-four head of cattle, on the hoof, from Badentoy to stock Glithno. They introduced two Ayrshire bulls, one of which gored Dod. Their flock of Border Leicester ewes was mated with Suffolk rams. I recall helping Dod to treat the flock for internal parasites, a precautionary measure. A phenolphthalein capsule was shot down each animal's throat by inserting a capsule in one end of a hosepipe twelve inches long and pushing a fifteen-inch stick through it. The term used was "drenching" the sheep.

Glithno was subsequently sold to two Wisely brothers, who had benefited when the road haulage firm Wm Wisely was nationalised. The brothers were vocally opposed to nationalisation on principle before learning how much they could gain financially. They saw an opportunity to invest in Glithno, although they were novices in farming. Dod happily agreed to stay and farm Glithno on their behalf.

Latterly, Dod lived next door to and worked at the Church of Scotland home for the elderly at the top of Robert Street, Stonehaven. The building was formerly the Bay Hotel, renamed Clashfarquhar House when it was bought and donated to the Kirk by Jimmy Nicol, a local farmer and speculator, who lived to be 99. Dod and Dolly celebrated their golden wedding in July 1987. The occasion was celebrated by their five daughters, Helen ("Babs"), Anne, Pat, Jean and Gilly, son George, and most of their sixteen grandchildren and their (then) two great-grandchildren.

Dod assumed the management of Causeyport as his father grew old and less mobile. Dod was a dab hand at servicing machinery and farm implements. If he had not been a farmer's boy by circumstance, he might have been a blacksmith or engineer. I enjoyed Dod's good-natured company at Causeyport and later at Glithno. Dod was unusually strong and could fork great bundles of sheaves all day with no apparent effort. On one occasion, I attempted to weigh him on the hanging balance used to weigh sacks of corn in the mill barn at Causeyport, but the available 20 stone of weights was not sufficient to tip the balance. Not surprisingly, he was anchor man in the Howe o' the Mearns tug-of-war team which competed at games meetings against the famous Bell's family team.

Dod employed me for the hairst at Glithno while I was on vacation from Aberdeen University. After a day in the fields, Dod and I occasionally slaked our thirst in a licensed grocer's back shop at Rickarton. Gamekeepers, beaters, poachers, farm labourers and other locals congregated in that howff. Another visitor was a repulsive bookie from Aberdeen who rented the local shooting lodge. Observing that the bookie had a case of whisky in the boot of his Armstrong Siddeley, the assembled sycophants hailed him as the great man who had taken a chance in life. (Perhaps he had absconded with the betting slips.) One toady said that the bookie was so rich that he did not have to live with his wife! The expressed admiration for this foul-mouthed and obnoxious bookie increased exponentially as he decanted drams all around. Dod and I reserved our opinions, accepted a dram and enjoyed the banter. Another time, Dod and I attended a concert party in Stonehaven, where we heard Robert Wilson lilt "The Bonnie Lass o' Ballochmyle" among other traditional and comical turns by his concert party.

Dod always expressed an interest in my studies and insisted that I justify my work. Once, I tried to justify a genetic experiment which involved incubating thousands of *Drosophila*, fruit flies, in milk bottles in the basement of Marischal College. Dod's profound response, "You cannot milk flies", may have influenced my choice of career. I learned from him that some of his children were taught science by my old schoolfriend and fellow student, Alistair Henderson, at the Mackie Academy, Stonehaven. I immediately thought of Burns' "On a Schoolmaster":

> Gi'e him the schoolin' o' your weans,
> For clever de'ils he'll mak' 'em!

My mother never understood why I went off to do research while I could have followed a respectable teaching career like Alistair H. She could then have explained what I did. Obviously, Mother did not know Alistair as I did.

Uncle Dod died in March 1991 aged 84. Auntie Dolly spent her last years in a sheltered flat at Brickfield, near Stonehaven railway station, and died in 1999 aged 85.

7/7 Williamina (Auntie Mina)

Causey hoped that their seventh-born would be a son. Granny said: "Aye, anither loon for ye tae fecht wi'" – but the last child turned out to be a girl, Williamina, not William, who nonetheless grew up to be a great favourite of her father because she was big and strong and had no qualms about doing "a loon's wark" on the farm. In December 1934, Mina married James "Aixie" Masson, a salmon fisherman who had a share of a coble. They lived in a thick-walled coastguard house on top of the cliffs at Catterline. Mina was always warmly welcomed by her father, particularly so when she brought him his favourite delicacy, a partan (edible crab). Aixie served in the Royal Navy during the 1939–45 war, while Mina returned to Causeyport with her young family to help with the milking and farm work along with her sister, Mary.

Auntie Mina lived latterly at 46 Fonthill Road, Aberdeen, where I visited her and members of her family on the evening of the day of Mary's funeral. Mina was in bed and did not seem to be perturbed about her dear sister's death. She recalled happy days at Causeyport, and laughed as she told me, without any rancour, that Annie, standing by a wooden sink, up to her elbows in soap suds, gave the youthful Mina a good hard soapy slap about the lugs to stop her larking about and start to share in the work. Our mother was fifteen years older than Mina, who told me that she was warned to be on good behaviour whenever Sam Jamieson visited Causeyport.

Mina died on 1st April 1998, aged 88, and the funeral was private. The four Masson children are Margaret, James, Audrey and Norman, and there are many descendants. Mina was the youngest and the last surviving member of the Alexander family from Causeyport.

"One generation passeth away,
and another generation cometh:
but the earth abideth forever".

Ecclesiastes, 1 v. 4

Glossary

(with acknowledgement to *The Concise Scots Dictionary*, Aberdeen: AUP, 1987)

bairn	young child
ben	through; towards the inner part of
blaeberries	blueberries
bothy	a separate building with living quarters for single workmen
boxmaster	treasurer
brae	a slope, incline
brambles	blackberries
bree	water in which anything has been boiled
breid	oatcake
brookie	grimy, dirty
bubblie jock	turkey cock
byre	cowshed
caff	chaff
cast	cut and dig out (peats)
causey	granite sett or cobblestone for roads and pavements
chaumer	sleeping quarters for farm workers, sometimes in a stable loft
chucken	chick
clocker	broody hen
clootie	enclosed in a cloth; made of cloth rags
close	farmyard
cole	haycock
coo	cow (plural: kye)
coobailie	cattleman
corn	oats
cottar	married farm worker occupying a cottage as part of his contract
cowts	colts
craws	crows
cutter	hip flask for half a mutchkin (0.43 litre) of whisky
dandy	stiff brush for grooming horses
deem	unmarried kitchen maid on a farm
de'il	devil
dominie	schoolmaster

doo	pigeon
doocot	dovecot
dook	bathe, plunge
draff	refuse of brewed malt
drenching	medicating
dry-stane	dry stone
dungers	dungarees
dux	top pupil
dyke	wall (not a ditch)
emmerteens	ants
feart	afraid
fecht	fight
fee	engagement of a farm servant for six months
fly cup	tea break
foun	to form the foundation of
galluses	braces for holding up trousers
gey	very
girnel	storage chest for oatmeal
glaur	sticky mud
greep	gutter in a byre
grieve	farm bailiff
haims	the two curved pieces of wood or metal covering or forming a horse-collar
hairst	harvest
hal twal	"half [of] twelve", i.e. half-past eleven
haud	hold
haver	talk at length, talk nonsense
heck	slatted wooden rack
hing in	hold on
howff	meeting place, pub, haunt
hummel	naturally hornless
hurl	convey in a wheeled vehicle
hyowin	hoeing
kebbock	whole cheese
kirk	church
kist	(wooden) chest
kittle	give birth to kittens
kye	cattle (plural of coo)

lade	mill-race	skirlie	fried oatmeal and onions
langstane	standing stone	slap	gap in a wall, fence or hedge
leerie	lamplighter	smiddie	blacksmith; smithy
loon	boy; young farm worker or odd-job boy	sonsie	comely
		souse	to pickle
		spug	sparrow
mains	a home farm, usually near a "big hoose" (great house)	steading	farm buildings, usually U-shaped and not including the farmhouse
mealie	made of oatmeal		
midden	dunghill or compost heap	stirk	bullock (or heifer)
moss	moorland area allocated for cutting peats	stour	dust, dirt
		stovies	stoved potatoes
muckle	large	strang	seepage
		swack	lithe, nimble, active
neep	turnip	swingle	chain and hook attached to a swye for hanging utensils
nickie-tams	straps or string worn below the knees to keep the trouser-leg lifted clear in dirty work or to exclude dust, vermin and so on		
		swye	movable iron bar above a fire supporting a swingle
orraman	odd-job man	tacketie	hobnailed
oxter	armpit; space under the upper arm	tamoshanter	Scottish flat round woollen hat with a central toorie
		tattie	potato
partan	edible crab (*Cancer pagurus*)	tawse	leather strap, formerly used for corporal punishment in Scottish schools
phaeton	four-wheeled open carriage		
primsie	prim, prudish, strait-laced		
rax	reach or stretch; strain or sprain	thrash	thresh
ree	chicken run	thraw	twist
roup	sale by auction	toonser	town-dweller
rowie	high-cholesterol flaky bread roll	toorie	tuft or bobble on a bonnet
ruck	hay- or corn-stack	tortie	tortoiseshell (cat)
		tracer	trace-horse
scaffie cairt	street-sweeper's cart	travis	wooden partition between stalls in a stable
scull	shallow basket		
scunner	feel nauseated, annoyed or bored	vricht	wright
sharn	cattle excrement	wapenshaw	rifle-shooting competition
sharp	frost-nail	wean	child
sheetin	shooting	whins	gorse
shelt	nimble horse	whisht!	quiet!
showd	to move with a rocking gait	whitrat	weasel
siclike	suchlike, similar	yirned milk	junket
skink	soup made from shin of beef		

Table 1
Auld Causey's forebears

Gen.
no.

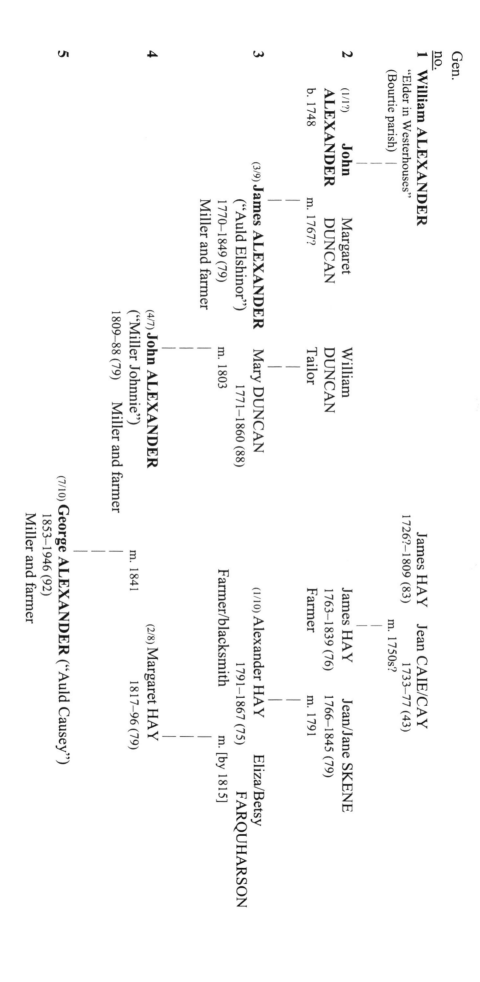

1 **William ALEXANDER**
"Elder in Westerhouses"
(Bourtie parish)

2 (1/1?) **John ALEXANDER**
b. 1748

    Margaret DUNCAN
    m. 1767?

    William DUNCAN
    Tailor

3 (3/9) **James ALEXANDER**
("Auld Elshinor")
1770–1849 (79)
Miller and farmer

    Mary DUNCAN
    1771–1860 (88)
    m. 1803

James HAY   Jean CAIE/CAY
1726?–1809 (83)   1733–77 (43)
          m. 1750s?

James HAY   Jean/Jane SKENE
1763–1839 (76)   1766–1845 (79)
Farmer   m. 1791

4 (4/7) **John ALEXANDER**
("Miller Johnnie")
1809–88 (79)
Miller and farmer

(1/10) Alexander HAY   Eliza/Betsy
1791–1867 (75)   FARQUHARSON
Farmer/blacksmith   m. [by 1815]

    (2/8) Margaret HAY
    1817–96 (79)
    m. 1841

5 (7/10) **George ALEXANDER** ("Auld Causey")
1853–1946 (92)
Miller and farmer

The generations are numbered in descending order of seniority from the earliest so far identified. My grandparents are in generation "5". The fractional convention "7/10" shows the parity of Causey's birth (7) and the total number of siblings born (10).

Table 2
Granny's forebears

Gen.
no.

1

John	James	Alexander	James Margaret Alexander Agnes	John Agnes	Robert Elizabeth	James Margaret	James
Ann	Margaret						
RITCHIE BIRNIE	REID HAY	GREIG + [?]	SMITH MORRICE	CARR LEIPER	MOLLISON WEBSTER	PATERSON DAVIDSON	WALKER CLARK
m. 1779	m.1786		m.	m.	m. 1781	m. 1772?	m. 1777

2

John RITCHIE 1787–1861 (74)	Mary GREIG 1782–1831 (49)	James REID d. 1871 (79)	Margaret SMITH d. 1872 (76)	John CARR 1783–1812 (28)	Elizabeth MOLLISON d. 1833 (47)	Robert PATERSON 1787–1858 (71)	Mary WALKER d. 1875 (80?)
m. 1813		m. 1818		m. 1807		m. 1829	

3

3/4 **David RITCHIE** (3/9) 1818–99 (80) — Jane/Jean REID 1824–80 (56)   m. 1841

3/3 John CARR 1812–87 (75) — 1/4 Ann PATERSON 1821–1915 (93)   m. 1850

4

4/10 **William Alexander RITCHIE** 1848–1917 (69) — 1/3 Ann CARR 1851–1915 (63)   m. 1871

5

1/8 **Ann Paterson RITCHIE** (Mrs ALEXANDER) 1872–1961 (89)

As in Table 1, my grandparents are in generation "5", following the system of numbering created by the software used by Ivor.

Four consecutive generations of firstborns, all called Ann. Left to right: Ann Paterson (Mrs Carr), Ann Paterson Alexander (later Mrs Jamieson), Ann Paterson Ritchie (Mrs Alexander), Ann Carr (Mrs Ritchie) (c. 1900).

Table 3
Seven siblings

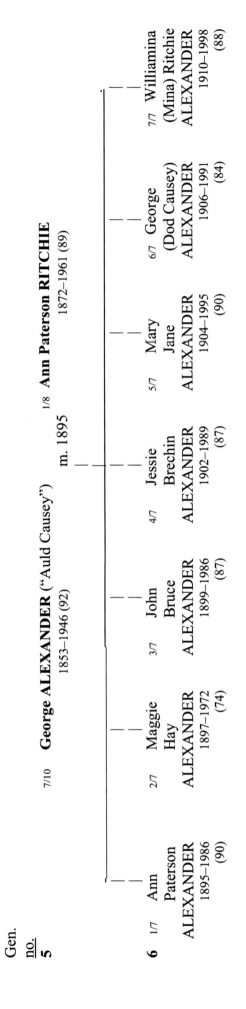

Gen.
no.

5

7/10 **George ALEXANDER** ("Auld Causey")
1853–1946 (92)

m. 1895

1/8 **Ann Paterson RITCHIE**
1872–1961 (89)

6

1/7 Ann
Paterson
ALEXANDER
1895–1986
(90)

2/7 Maggie
Hay
ALEXANDER
1897–1972
(74)

3/7 John
Bruce
ALEXANDER
1899–1986
(87)

4/7 Jessie
Brechin
ALEXANDER
1902–1989
(87)

5/7 Mary
Jane
ALEXANDER
1904–1995
(90)

6/7 George
(Dod Causey)
ALEXANDER
1906–1991
(84)

7/7 Williamina
(Mina) Ritchie
ALEXANDER
1910–1998
(88)

Average lifespan: 86.8 years (parents and offspring combined)

As in Tables 1 and 2, my grandparents are in generation "5", hence their seven children are in generation "6".

50

Index

Photograph of the author as a young man